FROM THE
PLANTATION
TO ME

PALMETTO
P U B L I S H I N G
Charleston, SC
www.PalmettoPublishing.com

Copyright © 2024 by James A Golden

All rights reserved

No portion of this book may be reproduced, stored in a retrieval system, or transmitted in any form by any means–electronic, mechanical, photocopy, recording, or other–except for brief quotations in printed reviews, without prior permission of the author.

Hardcover ISBN: 9798822957978
Paperback ISBN: 9798822957961
eBook ISBN: 9798822957985

FROM THE PLANTATION TO ME

AN AMERICAN STORY

JAMES A GOLDEN

DEDICATION

As a writer I pondered the idea of whether it would be a benefit to others my writing this book or if it would just turn out to be something for family discussions. But as I continued to write I began to realize that this was not just my story, it's and American story.

I was amazed and inspired by my grandfather. When I look back at the time I spent with him I even to this day I rely on the wisdom he brought into my life. He was the CEO and his farm was his corporation even though he signed his name with an X he ran his business like a wise man. By today"s terms he would be a top ranked businessman. Yet he was compassionate, caring and showed great concern for his fellows.

I was not quite sure at the time of just what it was that I was witnessing as I traveled to market or tried to work the fields as he did. But later in my life the skills he was teaching me would help me tremendously in business and in life.

Our talks after and incident where he a grown man was called boy or words even worst he would calm me down. He taught me that even when the world doesn't seem nice that should not turn me bitter.

So as you read this book, look for the similarity to your story. Is there someone who you still reflect on when you've done something because they taught you how. Do you find yourself doing something and afterward saying I remember where I learned that, if so your story is like my story a bunch of things I've learned from those who came before me.

I dedicate this book to anyone who dears to look at where they came from with a mind set on learning and becoming better for having done so.

I dedicate this to my father who was my hero, my grandfather my mentor and to my family and friends.

To my brother Richard: I did not forget you.

To my God the author of my life.

FOREWORD

Have you ever wondered why you look a certain way or have a certain mannerism? Have you ever looked in the mirror and wondered where you got those dimples or those brown (or whatever color) eyes you have? Was there ever a time when you wondered where you came from and what your ancestors had to go through just to make it possible for you to even be here? If you have and like me you allowed the opportunity to get the right answers slip away, don't be discouraged; there may still be some hope for you. With all the resources of this day and age, the opportunity could very well still exist.

I allowed a whole lifetime to pass by before I realized I wanted to know more about people whom I admired or even shaped some of my life. Not to mention that there was ample time at various times in my life when I had the opportunity to be with them yet feared asking about their lives or getting to know them better. Perhaps it was out of fear that I remained silent at those times; perhaps it was my youth that didn't allow me to think that some day they would no longer be there to ask questions of. Perhaps it was my upbringing, during which it was stated children did not question their elders. I cannot place a good reason on why it took so long, but I'm thankful that there is still time, and that time is now.

As a child from New York City, I got the opportunity to live on a farm for a while. If I were to be totally honest with myself, I would admit that my life changed as a result of that visit and the longer period of time that I spent on that farm. The shocker wasn't the city-boy-living-in-the-country aspect; it wasn't even the lifestyle change. What it was, even though I didn't realize it, was the man who I would learn to love. The man who would teach me some valuable life lessons. The man who would show me how to live in a society I had before then only heard of and thought very little about.

That man was my grandfather Cleveland Golden, the farm was in South Carolina, and it was the early 1960s. He was a black man at a time when even at his age, he would have been called boy. He owned a lot of land at a time when black folks I knew were renting apartments from white landlords in Harlem.

I got to see the following in him: As a farmer who worked his land by himself, he was a hard worker, and it paid off. As an employer, he treated people fairly and with respect. As a businessman, he stood up to those who wanted to cheat him. As a man, he had pride in his family and himself. All of these qualities I have used throughout my life. So even now I get to thank God for this man and the ability to tell his story. He was the smartest man I knew, and he signed his name with an X.

TABLE OF CONTENTS

Foreword vii

Part I: Chapter 1 1

Part II***: Chapter 2 31

Chapter 3 67

Chapter 4 93

Chapter 5 121

Chapter 6 143

Part III: Chapter 7 153

Chapter 8 175

Chapter 9 197

Chapter 10 219

Chapter 11 235

Chapter 12 261

Chapter 13 279

PART I

CHAPTER 1

1887

From the farmhouse the cry of the new infant's birth rang out. The woman stepped out onto the porch and announced, "It's a boy." The men gathered on the porch, walked over to the man staring upward at the heavens, and congratulated him. His name was Philip Golden; he was my great-grandfather. And born the fifteenth of May was Cleveland Golden, my grandfather.

Philip walked into the house and into the room where the child was born. The woman handed him the baby boy, wrapped in a tiny blanket, and he smiled as he looked at the healthy baby. This was his third male child and only the second since one had died shortly after birth four years earlier. After his examination of the child, he handed him back to the woman and went over to see about his wife. "You done fine," he said to the woman as she lay still on the sweat-drenched bed. "Yes, you done fine," he continued, then kissed her forehead and left the room.

Philip walked out the back door and over to the shade where the wine and moonshine were kept. He picked up a bottle of the clear liquid and made his way back to the kitchen, where he placed the bottle and five glasses on a tray. When he returned to the front porch, the men there greeted him eagerly. Each one grabbed a glass and waited for a word from the proud father.

"He looks good, and she's fine," Philip said as he poured himself a drink and passed the bottle. He waited until all of the men had drink in their glass. "God has blessed this family again," he went on as he lifted up his glass toward the other men.

Their glasses clinked, and they took a drink. "Amen," they said in unison, then took another drink.

1893

The woman's voice rang out, breaking the silence of the mornings breeze.

"Cleveland," she cried, "Cleveland, where are you boy?"

Philip could hear her even from the patch of field he was plowing some twenty-five yards away. He knew this was not the first time he had heard Carrie calling for Cleveland, and he had an idea just where to find him. He laid the plow down and made his way to the front of the cornfield he had planted just days ago. He was not surprised to see Cleveland sitting on the ground grabbing handfuls of dirt.

"Boy, what's you doing?" Philip asked as he moved closer to his young son. "You sho like the earth. I gots me a farmhand here," he continued.

Cleveland smiled as he saw his father coming toward him. He grabbed another handful of dirt and showed it to his dad.

"Yeah, I sees, you likes the earth, but I gotta get you back to your mama before she shouts her head off. I'll see 'bout rigging something up for you so you can come out in the field with me, but until then you have got to stay where your mama could see you sos she don't be worried 'bout you." He bent down and picked his son up and turned toward to house. "I got him, Carrie," he shouted. "I'm bringing him in now."

Three days later Philip went into the room of his young son and woke him up. "Do you want to go into the field with me?" he asked the boy, who by now was wiping the sleep out of his eyes. Cleveland shook his head up and down but was really not awake yet. "If you want to be a farmer, you have to get up early so that you can get a good bit done before it gets too hot to stand, boy," Philip continued. "Sos if you want to go with me, you gotta get up now. I'll be waiting in the kitchen for you, but I'll only wait a short time, so get up or go back to sleep. It's up to you."

Cleveland watched as his father walked out of the room. Even at his age he knew that this was an opportunity he didn't want to miss. He jumped out of bed and hurried to the outhouse. The sun was not quite up yet, but there was enough light to see his way clearly. He had never been up this early before and didn't realize that a farmer had to do it this way, but he was ready.

After about fifteen minutes, Cleveland came into the kitchen. To his surprise his mother was there also, and he could smell the hot biscuits that were baking in the wood oven. There, too, was bacon and eggs cooking on the stove; he didn't know that all this went on so early in the morning.

"Did you wash your face and hands?" his mother asked in a stern voice.

"Yes um," Cleveland answered. "I sho did."

"Well, then sit down and get ready for breakfast," she replied as she turned to check on the food on the stove.

"Where's papa?" he asked as he took his place at the table.

"He's in the front yard working on the gadget he made for you so that you can work with him fo' a while."

Just then Philip walked into the room carrying a horse harness with some straps on it. "This should do it," he said as held the thing up against his son. "Yep, this should do just fine."

After breakfast Philip rose up from the table and leaned over and kissed Carrie. He waited for Cleveland to get up and watched as he went over and kissed his mother

"Lets go, boy," he said, and they walked out the door. "I'll bring him back OK," he added as they headed for the patch of land off to the right of the farm. "I won't let nothing happen to him, I 'sures ya." They walked out of sight.

Philip put the harness around his son and the straps around himself; this allowed Cleveland to stand just in front of him, and if the was a problem, he would be able to lift Cleveland up an even dislodge him if the mule was to try to take off. Philip explained to his son that they would be plowing a path down and back up from end to end. Cleveland was excited and ready to go.

They plowed an acre before long. Cleveland was a natural. He was surely a farmer—he enjoyed every bit of it.

When it was time for him to go home, he didn't want to quit. "I'll bring you back tomorrow," Philip promised, "but you need to go to the house now or your mama will be mad at me." Philip removed the harness and lifted his son up. He could see the tears in his eyes but he knew he didn't want to anger Carrie.

The next days and weeks were just the same, except that over time, Cleveland was allowed to stay out later. By the end of the planting season, Cleveland would go to the fields just to see how the buds were coming out of the ground. There was something about looking at the earth you had toiled and seeing the result. He would walk, just to make sure that at each place he had put a seed, there was something coming up. He would spend hours just walking up and down each row.

Carrie had long since stopped calling for her son when he was not around. She pretty much knew just where he was, looking over the fields he and his daddy had planted. She asked him to come in for lunch but didn't get upset when he was a little late. His sister Anna or his brother Johnnie would go to the fields and call him in.

Philip was proud, too, seeing the reaction of his youngest son to farming. He had hoped that Johnnie would show such interest but he didn't take to it like Cleveland did, even though Johnnie was good with the livestock and he sure was good with the horses. That boy could outride any of them, so he did show his place on the farm.

He and Anna held up their end of keeping the farm going with milking and such. Heck, Philip had nothing to complain about at all. God had blessed him with a good family, and their land was free and clear so all that they worked for was theirs to keep. He did, however, from time to time remember what he had been told by his father, Philip Sr., about those early days before they were freed.

Philip Sr. did not want his family to go through life not knowing that there was a price to pay for freedom. He would sit around the kitchen table and tell the story of how he and his wife Rebeca first saw each other while working on the Golding Plantation.

Yes, he wanted them to know that there were some hard times associated with their lives. "Heck, Master Golding was downright hateful at times," he would say, "up until that day when the horse throwed him. And he laid there in them woods for two days."

Philip could hear him now.

1843

This had to be the hottest day ever, Philip thought. He had been working the field and planting cottonseed. It was like the devil was breathing hot air from hell itself over the land. The earth was so dry he wondered why they were even trying to plant anything in this kind of weather.

Philip had been farming and tending to horses on this plantation ever since he was sold to Master Golding, when he was about eleven or twelve years old. He knew when it was a good time to plant, and this surely was not one. He related, "But master had said to plant now, so there was nothing left to say. After we plowed and put down seed, the master had us all form a line, with one person pumping water from the well and the rest of us toting water to the field. This was backbreaking work since there were over five acres and God only knows how many rows to water. We worked straight into night before we got the whole field done."

He was making his way back to his cabin when he spotted a young pretty black woman carrying a pail of water, spilling it as she made her way past him. He was really wanting to go to his cabin, where he could get some rest after the hard day he had had, but instead he called out to her.

"Hey, I think you might be needing some help with that," he said. "I don't know why yo' man didn't think that too."

"Maybe I ain't got no man," she answered, "and can tote my water myself." She walked ahead, still spilling the water with every step.

"I reckon you won't have any water in the pail by the time you get to where you're going," Philip said as he caught up to her and placed his hand on the pail, touching hers slightly.

"If you want to, I guess it's OK," she said, adding, "I surely don't need the help, though."

"I'm pleased to do it, pretty lady," he said, "and by the way, what's yo' name?"

"It's surely not 'pretty lady'; it's Rebeca."

"Why, it's my pleasure to meet you, Ms. Rebeca," he said as they made their way to her cabin. It was clear aways from his, and he knew he had better get in before there was hell to pay. He placed the pail of water before the front door of her cabin and bade her good night. He could not get her out of his mind the whole walk to his cabin; he knew he wanted to see her again.

Philip woke earlier than the usual time of sunup. He realized that he hadn't slept very well; he had thought about Rebeca all night. He wondered how it was that he had never seen her before. He pretty much knew every slave on the plantation, yet he couldn't think of a time or place that he'd seen her, and he knew he would have remembered her if he had.

Now that he knew where her cabin was, he had to figure a way to cross paths with her again. It couldn't be by going over there since that was a place set aside for young women and children. It was on the way to the stables, and he had plenty of access to them most of the week. That would have to be how he got information on Rebeca. Maybe he'd see her on her way to or from the stables and could get her attention. He already knew that she was allowed out to gather water; maybe she had other chores that would get her away from that area. It would be too dangerous to just go there, but if nothing else panned out, he knew he would risk it—he wanted to see her that badly, and nothing was going to stop him, not even a lashing.

Philip washed his face in the cold well water and set out toward the stables. It was now sunup, and the roasters were crowing. It was near time for the slaves to get up and get ready for a hard day's work. As he came closer to the cabins that the woman and children stayed in, he slowed down his pace. He was hoping that she would be up and about even though he knew it was very early. As he got nearer to the cabin, he walked her to last night, he was all but crawling, his steps almost dragging. Hell, he might as well have just stopped walking altogether.

Just as he was about to give up, he spotted Rebeca. She again had a pail in her hand. She was coming from behind the cabin and heading toward the well off to the right. He knew that if he stepped up his pace, he could catch up with her just before she got to the well, so he did.

Arriving just behind her, he called out to her. "Good morning, Ms. Rebeca," he said, trying to hide the excitement in his voice.

"Good morning to you too," she replied, realizing that she didn't know his name.

"I 'spect you'd be wasting water again," he said with a smile on his face.

"Sir, I've been toting water long before I got that little bit of help from you yesterday just fine, thank you," she answered.

"I'm sure you have, and the thirsty ground sho is glad when you do. I'm going to the stables, so I'll only be able to help you half the way back," he said.

"Didn't you hear me? I don't need no help from you," she said.

"I know," Philip said as he took the pail from her hand.

"What's yo' name?" Rebeca asked.

"My name Philip," he answered as they approached the well, "and you's gonna be my woman."

"No I ain't," Rebeca said with a slight smile on her face.

For the next few months, they would meet in the morning when he worked the stables and, in the evening, when he worked the farm. Their time together grew into love, and they knew that they wanted to spend their lives together even if it was in the condition that they were in, so Philip approached Master and asked for her hand in marriage.

Master had always kinda taken a liking to Philip, probably because he was such a good horseman and could always be counted on to help out wherever needed without complaining or slacking. Master had no problem granting Philip and Rebeca's union in marriage, so they were allowed to marry and move into a cabin of their own.

Then came that day when Master went riding and the horse came back without him. Heck, everybody was in and uproar. The overseers went out looking for him, spending hours and finding no sign of him anywhere. The second day they continued the search and still couldn't find him. Philip and Master had gone riding before and had gone to areas that no one else had, so Philip asked if he could join in the search. Everyone knew that he was a good horseman and that he had been known to ride with Master in the past, so they agreed to let him join the search.

Philip road into a heavily wooded area. He remembered a large tree that stood out from all the others. He and master had been there before. He looked at the ground and could see that the leaves been crumbled and flattened as if something large had been crawling along the area. Philip stopped and listened to the sounds of the woods and soon recognized the muffled noise of someone moaning. He headed toward the sound and soon saw the outline of a large man on the ground. It was Master, and he was in pretty bad shape.

Philip rushed over to him and could see right away that his leg was broken; he also had a large scar on his neck, down to his back. Philip spoke to Master and assured him that he would be all right as he began to tend to his wounds first. He wrapped cloth around the neck wounds and began searching for wood to create splints for the broken leg.

"I'll be right back, Master," Philip said to the wounded man, who could hardly speak. "Don't you worry 'bout a thing. I gots ya, and we's gonna get you home directly."

He walked away to search for the wood. Within minutes Philip returned with the wood and placed it on each side of Master's leg. He tore off pieces of his trousers and wrapped the wood tightly around the leg until it was a sturdy addition and support.

"OK, Master, now I'm gonna need you to help out. Now I knows it's gonna hurt, but I gots ta get you up and on the horse so you gotta stand up," Philip said as he reached down to the wounded man, still lying on the ground. "Now put yo' arms around my neck, and as I stand, you stand."

Master did just as he was told, and before long they were both standing near the horse. "Now put your good foot into the stirrup, and I'm gonna help you to pull yourself up," Philip said.

Again Master did exactly what he was told, and he was up over the horse. "Now, again, this is gonna hurt, but I gotta pull your leg over the horse and get you sitting up right," Philip said, looking for the wounded man's approval. "Are you ready?"

Master shook his head in agreement, and Philip took the broken leg and pulled it over to the other side of the horse as the wounded man cried out in pain. "You did good, Master," Philip said. "You'll be home shortly." It took another two hours before they reached the big house.

A month later Master gave Philip and Rebeca their freedom.

"Are you daydreaming again?" the woman's voice asked. "I've been calling you for some time now. Heck, I thought you were out in the fields again, and here you are just sitting on the porch napping. Wes having company over this weekend, and I wanted to ask you to get me a ham out the smokehouse so I can get it ready for cooking. I'll make two apple pies and a pound cake, since I knows yo'sister likes my pies."

"All right, Rebeca Philip answered. "I'll bring in the ham and a jug of that grape wine I made too. We can all sip on that he continued. Oh, where is Cleveland? He can walk with me to the smokehouse."

"I saw that boy standing by the fields you and he planted. He may still be out that way."

Philip called out the young boy's names twice before Cleveland called back from the field. "Come give me a hand," Philip called out to the boy, who was by then running toward the house.

"I'm here, Papa," the young boy said as he entered the porch area.

Philip smiled. He could see the look of excitement in the young boy's eyes; he knew that Cleveland liked being with him.

Together they retrieved the items from the smokehouse and brought them to the kitchen. It was almost time for supper, and Cleveland could smell the fresh baked bread still in the oven. All of a sudden, he realized that he was hungry. "I'll go wash up," he said. "It sure smells good in here."

Both Carrie and Philip laughed as they watched their young son leave the room. "That boy something else," Carrie said.

"Yeah, I 'spect you right," Philip said as they continued laughing.

1898

Carrie called out in her loudest voice, letting the men know that it was time for them to come in for lunch. She had placed the meal on the table and wanted them to eat while it was still hot. Those two so loved the land that they would stay out there in all that sun from sunup till sundown if she didn't make sure that they came in for a break to get out of that sun and eat something.

Philip came into the kitchen first which, was always the case. He was drying himself off after washing up. A few minutes later, Cleveland came into the kitchen area; he, too, was drying himself off.

Carrie watched as the two men began to eat. She could tell that they were both hungry but if she had not called to them, they would still be out in the field. When the plates were almost clean, the two men began to speak to one another.

"How's it going over there?" Philip asked his young son, who now was framing seven acres on his own.

"I finished planting an acre of watermelon yesterday. Should be finished planting two acres of corn before sunset today. I still have to turn the soil where the okra and the peanuts were planted for the past three years. After that maybe you can come over and we can figure out what to plant there or if maybe we should let the land rest for a season."

Philip was amazed at how his young son had taken to farming, to the extent that he even knew that land had to rest if the same items were planted on it from year to year. "I'll make it a point to get over there as soon as you are finished turning the soil. It will be easier for me to make a call on what to do after I see what it looks like after turning," he said while looking at his young son's face. How serious he was about the land. "We'll figure it out together."

"Yes sir," Cleveland answered, taking his last bite.

PART II***

Cleveland

The planting was all done, and there was a short break in farming chores as the crops began to peek through the ground. The weather also seemed to want to cooperate; we got a good supply of rain for the season. Papa went to making wine for the holiday season, and I picked fresh fruit for Mama to make preserves. There were also pecans to be harvested and put away.

I grew weary. I liked planting more than anything else; there was nothing better than the smell of freshly turned soil and watching as a bud turned into a harvest of corn or melons or beans or tatas.

One day a heap of birds came 'round the farm. Papa said we had to scare them birds off or they'd eat all our crop if it was able to grow enough to give fruit.

Papa and I would get up early and go to the field wit' the shotgun and my pellet gun, and we'd shoot them birds dead. That would have been fun just like hunting, sep we got up before sunrise and I never liked doing that.

All in all, the season went well. There was also the excitement of going to town and selling off some of the crops. We took melons, cucumbers, and peanuts to the marketplace, where Papa talked with the white folks and they gave him money and took the crops off the wagon.

It was only the second time I had come with Papa. I didn't really like going to town; there was something bout the way them white folks looked at papa and me. I don't think they liked us very much, but Papa would smile at them and say few words and take the money that they handed him. When we got home, he would take the money outta his pocket and put it in the metal box, then take it out back.

I never seed what he did with the metal box, but he didn't bring it back into the house until the next time he went to town wit' mo' crops. "You go and get cleaned up for supper, Cleveland," he said to me when he came back in the house. "It was a bit of a dusty ride to and from town."

"Yes, Papa," I said as I went out to the well.

Papa and me would make that trip many times during the harvest season. At times we'd take corn or berries, even tatas, and them white folks would do the same thing—look us over.

Papa would smile at them, shake his head, say a few words, then take the money, and they'd take the crops off the wagon, and we'd go home. I even think that over time I started to not really care that they looked at me as if they didn't want to see me; somehow all that really mattered was that Papa got the money and we got home in time for supper.

It was nearing the holiday season. I really liked this time of the year 'cuz we'd bring a small tree in the house and gather 'round it. Papa said it was a time to give thanks for what we had and to thank God for the year gone by for the fact that we had good health and food to eat and crops to sell. The only problem was that Mama was feeling herself, and she stayed in bed for most of the time.

We were not allowed to go in to see her. Papa said she needed her rest. I wasn't so sure that she was getting any rest, 'cuz I could hear her coughing a lot even when it was time for all of us to be sleeping. Papa stopped sleeping in there after a while, when the coughing got worse.

One day the wagon came, and they took Mama out of the house. I waited for her to come back, but after three days, Papa gathered us around the kitchen table and told us that Mama had passed. I wasn't so sure just what he meant by that, so I asked when she was coming back home. He told me that she was not coming back, and she had passed on. It wasn't until we had a service in the church, and I saw Mama laid in that box that I figured out what it meant to pass on.

Mama had died. Why didn't papa just say that? I thought. I had a dog that got kicked by the mule and it died. Nobody said to me that my dog had passed on; they said that the dog died, and after a while I got another dog. I knew that when something died, it wasn't coming back, like mama wasn't.

That holiday season was the worst one I ever had. None of us were as we used to be when Mama was here. There were no pies sitting near the window cooling off. The smell of fresh-baked ham or yams was not coming from the kitchen. Papa just sat around and drank from the clear stuff he kept in the shed. No one dared to say very much to him as he sat in silence. Some days his friends would come over and sit with him until he'd tell them to go home and leave him alone. This was surely the worst time this house had ever seen, until one day Papa wasn't sitting around anymore. I asked where he had gone, and the best answer I could get was he went out.

I checked the stable and noticed that his horse was gone; Papa hadn't been out riding in a long time. This was different. There was something going on. After many hours of lookin' out the window, I saw Papa coming down the pathway. He looked larger that I ever remembered him being, and he surely looked better than he had sitting round the house for the past few weeks.

There would be many more days when Papa would be gone for most of the day. One day he took the wagon instead of the horse. That day she came into our lives. She had a good smile and seemed to want to get to know us since she asked questions of all of us, somehow knowing a little about us as she asked. I wondered why she had come and became very upset when she began to take Mama's pans out of the cupboard and put on one of Mama's aprons. I went to my room and stayed there until I was called to come to the kitchen. I didn't want to go, but it had been a long time since the kitchen smelled like that. If I didn't know better, I'd think that Mama was back from the dead; the smells made me hungry.

It had become a weekend thing, Ms. Clara coming to the house and cooking us meals. She was even good at baking cakes. One she made with sliced peaches—I really liked that one a lot. Then came the day we all knew was coming Papa announced that Ms. Clara was going to be moving in with us, and she was going to be our stepmother. He told us that we could still call her Ms. Clara and that she was not taking the place of Mama. It was more how they would be that would change.

Papa had given away most of Mama's things. Some he put in the shed behind the house. He hid them under some wood in the back corner of the shed; I happened to have seen them one day when I was looking for a piece of wood to use in the field.

I think he wanted to keep them without anyone knowing. It would be something that he could look at from time to time when he missed her the most. I never let on that I knew they were there, even when he asked me what I was doing with the wood and where I got it from. I still remember him calling out to me, "Cleveland, what is you doing with that wood, and where did you get it from?"

"I want to mark off a spot in the field that has a hole I'll fix later, and I got it from near the back porch," I answered. I didn't like lying to him, but I thought maybe I should just this once to keep his secret. I thought that I owed him that. I had also kept something: the comb that Mama used.

1900

Papa and Ms. Clara got married, and before long there was two new babies in the house and one on the way. I began to have a bad feeling about this, not because there was a baby coming but because the house wasn't getting any bigger yet mo' people was living in it. I was sure that before long some of us was going to have to move out of the house. I didn't want to be away from my farming chores; I really liked farming, and I felt that if I was sent away, I'd never get to do in no mo'.

Before long the baby was born. It was a girl, and they named her Sarah. I couldn't tell if Papa was happy having a girl or not—he didn't show it in any way.

Papa had a chance to buy the small farm down the road. He had had his eye on it for a while. It bordered a piece of land he already owned and was six acres around the large pond. His plan was to build another smaller house on it and to use the water from the pond to irrigate the land on either side of it.

One morning Papa got up early and rode into town. He was gone most of the day before he came into the house and called us all into the kitchen. He had got the land and was letting us know what was next.

"I'ma see what needs to be done to the house, and some of you will be living there," he said. "Concha gonna live there too and look after you two boys," he continued, looking at me and Johnnie. "It's right up the road a piece, so I 'spects ya to still come here to help out on this side until I figure out what all I wanna do with the land on that side.

"We's gonna start the work on the house next week. I want you and Johnnie to come with me so you can look the place over."

We both just nodded our heads up and down. There was really nothing else we could do. It was final: we were being removed from our house and going to another, even if it was just up the road.

The house turned out to be not so bad. We both ended up with bigger rooms, and we surely did like Aunt

Concha; she made the best peach cobbler. Papa said it would be ready in a few weeks, and we could hardly wait.

It took most two months before the house was ready, and though me and Johnnie was ready to move in, we had to wait for Papa to go and get Aunt Concha and all her stuff into the house first. That took another ten days. It seemed that she lived quite a while away, and with packing her stuff on the wagon and all, we just had to wait.

When we finally settled in, the real work started. Both Johnnie and I still had to make our way up the road to work the land and take care of the farm animals. This became quite a chore and soon took its toll on Johnnie. He and Papa became at odds with each other, and Johnnie began to think about leaving home. I looked up to Johnnie and didn't want to see him leave. I also wondered what his leaving would do to the farm, since he was so good with the horses and such, but it was becoming clearer that he was fidin' to leave and there was little that I could do to stop it from happening.

Several months of bickering between Papa and Johnnie transpired until one night Johnnie came into my room after a long day of work. He had made up his mind: he was moving south to Savannah. He wanted to try out something different; he wanted a new way of life for himself in the big city. That next morning, when I awoke and got ready to make my way to the fields on the big farm,

I looked into Johnnie's room, and he was gone. I don't remember if he told me goodbye or not. I guess even if he had, I wouldn't have wanted to believe it. Again, there was a sadness in me almost as strong as the one I had felt when Mama died. There was a hole, an emptiness; another piece of my life had been removed from me and couldn't be replaced.

I made my way down to papa's house, wondering just how to tell him that Johnnie was gone. When I got there, Papa had just finished breakfast. Ms. Clara offered me a plate, and I had sat down at the table, ready to tell Papa the bad news, when he asked if I was all right, knowing that Johnnie had left. I tried to understand whether Papa was upset or not; he was not showing the kinda reaction I thought he should, given that one of his sons had just up and left like that.

"I'm hurting, I said. "I never knowed a time when Johnnie was not around, and I don't know just what that is going to be like for me."

"It's just one of those things," Papa said, "when a man has to decide just what he wants to do with his life. I've had to do it, and at some point, you'll have to do it too. He's gonna be all right. I gave him a good horse and some money to get him started on his way, and he always had a good head about him, so I think he'll make out just fine. Now you eat up—we got a full day ahead of us."

"Yes, Papa, I answered, really wanting to hear mo' about Johnnie's and Papa's arrangement. Where did Johnnie go in Savannah? Who was he staying with there? Did we have kinfolk that I didn't know about in Savannah? My po' head was bursting with questions, all of which papa wasn't giving me any answers to. Maybe after a while, when Papa mo' relaxed, I'll get a chance to get some answers to the questions in my head, I thought.

We worked the upper field, Papa on one end and me on the other. The land had to be plowed and turned, so that we could use it later fo' planting. By the time we were finished, I was so tired all I wanted to do was eat me a meal and get me some sleep; there was not gonna be any talking tonight about Johnnie or anything else. I went to the backyard and washed up, hollered into the house that I'd see them in the morning, and started my walk up the road to the house. I knew that Auntie would like company.

1904

Johnnie had come to visit Papa and all of us several times over the past year. He had been doing well. On his last visit he was driving a motorcar; it was the greatest thing I had ever seen. There were white folk in town riding in motor cars, but to see Johnnie riding one was something special fo' me to see. Right then the seed was planted deep in my mind: as much as I loved working the farm, I now wanted to see what it was like in the big city. I wanted to go to Savannah. It was my time, I felt.

Papa had brought even mo' land, and I feared that it would just be too much for him to handle on his own. Even though he would from time to time hire them Johnson boys to help out, I knew that my part was also very important for the place. Papa did tell me some time ago that I would have to make my own decisions about what I wanted to do with my life when the time came, but I still didn't know how to tell him that I wanted to leave the farm, the one place that I had learned so much from, the place that taught me how to use the land for good. This was not gonna be easy. In fact, it was going to be the hardest thing I had ever had to do.

One day at the well, Papa must have seen something in my face telling him I had had wanting to leave on my mind for weeks. "Son, what's eating at ya?" he asked in a bold and direct voice. "You been moping around here for some time now."

"Papa, I been thinking that I may want to…" At that point the words got stuck in my throat. I couldn't' seem to finish what I wanted to say.

"Cleveland, I've been noticing you dragging yo'self round for weeks now. I was waiting for you to tell me what was going on with you, but you didn't say a word. Now is as good a time as any to get it off yo' chest," Papa said. "So come on out with it, Son. I got a feeling I know what's going on, but I can't be sho until you say so."

"Papa, I just been feeling like I need a change, I'm a man now, and seein' how Johnnie went off and found his way, I think it's about my turn. I don't think that Uma need anything from you sepin a ride ta the train. I been savin' my money just in case I ever decided to make a move like this."

"Hold back a minute," Papa said, "movin' from what you know to what you don't know is not as easy as you may think it is. I made a lot of arrangements before Johnnie left this household. I'll make some for you, too, before you leave. I don't mind you going, but I won't let my child go into that world without help to get by, whether or not it's needed."

I tried to read Papa's face to see iffin he was angry with me fo' wanting to leave home, but from what I could tell, it didn't bother him much at all. He might even have been a bit happy that I was about to go out into the world and fend fo' myself.

"I'll let you know in about two or so weeks what I've come up with," Papa said. "You just continue with your chores until then. Oh, just in case yo' wondering, I'm proud of you, Son, and I think you'll learn yo'self pretty well. Now maybe you can stop the moping around you been doing and put some joy on that face." With that, we parted ways.

CHAPTER 2

1912

The day was near. Papa had made some arrangements fo' me to stay with an old friend of his. He thought it would be better for me than staying with Johnnie, even though Johnnie said it would be all right for me to stay with him. Papa said that Johnnie had ways, and it was just better for me not to be in between that. I wasn't sure I understood any of that, but fo' me, it was OK just to finally be getting on my way.

It had seemed like forever since Papa and me had our talk about me leaving. It had really only took him two weeks to get all this set up fo' me. I was gonna take a train to Savannah, and this friend would meet me at the station.

I was packed and ready four days before. Papa put some folding money in a handkerchief and told me to use it wisely. I put it into the pocket of the pants I was going to wear and left it there. I had saved pocket change of $3.15 and folding money of $4.00. I was sure that I had enough to last me for a while.

We had a nice meal at Papa's house the night before I was to leave. Ms. Clara cooked ham and baked a cake. Aunt Concha made some peach cobbler. It was a fine meal fo' a send-off. I was told that there would be some ham sandwiches fo' me to take on my train ride and of course a nice chunk of cake. I ate till I felt like I was almost about to bust wide open before Papa took me into the living room, where he began to tell me what to look out for.

He said that there were bad people in the big city and that I was to watch out fo' where I be and who be 'round me. He said that people bumped into you and picked yo' pocket so I was to keep my money in my front pocket, where they couldn't just take it form me. He said that I was not to go to bars and places where there was a lot of drinking going on 'cause folk get drunk and fight in those places. Then he talked about the women; he said be careful what women you take up wit'. He said that some women were just put to take yo' money and some could make you real sick if you lay with them. I was not so sure just what Papa was doing telling me all this, but somehow, I felt that it was worth me listening to, so I paid close attention to every word he was saying. After a while he ended his talk by saying just be careful in whatever you do, and you'll be just fine.

I left to go to the other house with a lot on my mind. There was all that papa said, and there was the excitement of leaving in the morning, I was not going to sleep very much that evening, that was fo' sho.

Somehow, I did manage to sleep quite well. I woke up at sunup, which was not unlike any other day. I rushed out to the well to draw a pail of water so I could wash up really good for my trip. When I came back into the house, Aunt Concha was up and about. At that moment I realized that I was leaving her alone in this house. I also realized that I was going to miss her and Papa, and Ms. Clara. Heck, I was going to miss this place and everybody in it.

Aunt Concha had made a fire in the stove and was beginning to cook me some breakfast. I really wanted to go over to the other house but though it better to stay and have breakfast with her for the last time. She made crackling' bread and eggs and bacon; I became hungry just from the smells that were coming outta the kitchen. I ran to my seat when she called me to come to eat. After the meal I thanked Aunt Concha fo' fixing such a good breakfast. I was glad that I stayed and a little sad that I was leaving.

My train was leaving at twelve thirty. I said my goodbyes to Aunt Concha and went over to the big house. I didn't know what time it was, but I knew it was nowhere near noon 'cause the sun was still down. Papa was sitting out on the porch when I got there, and he looked me over pretty well before he told me to go in the house and say goodbye to the rest of the family. It finally felt real after I gave hugs and said my goodbyes to everyone. I was going away, away from home, for the very first time.

It was a short while before Papa went to the barn and began to hitch the horse to the carriage. The ride to the station was a pretty long one. I grabbed my bag and put it into the wagon while Papa went in the house. When he returned, it was time to go. Everyone was out on the porch. They all were waving toward me, and I didn't eat them to see that I was crying. This was goodbye.

Papa didn't say much during the ride; I didn't have much to say either. We both just looked at the scenery and straight ahead. Before long I could see the small station house. It was not much to look at. In fact, it was a kind of run-down place, especially the part where colored folk waited to catch the train.

We got there a bit early, and Papa, I knew, had to get back to the farm. He took my bag out the wagon and walked with me to the place where I got my ticket. "Now you just remember what I told you about the big city," he said. "An' mine yo' own business, and you'll be just fine. Mr. Brown will meet you at the station; he's a chubby little man with a big smile. When you get off the train, just follow the colored folks and look out for him. I told him what you look like and what you'd be wearing. There should be no problem. If he's not there, you just stay there until he comes for you." He handed me my bag and my ticket. "You take care of yo'self," he continued, "and iffin you want to come home, you just tell Mr. Brown, and I'll send for you." He gave me a hug. And he didn't say bye; he just walked out the door to the wagon.

A train came to the station, but it was going north; I was to catch the train going south to Savannah. As I sat there wait fo' my train, I watched as a colored man in a dark-blue suit moved around the station. He would pick up bags fo' white folks and walk them to the train or from the train, and they would reach into their pocket and give him some spending change. If that man was to do that all day and folk just gave him spending change like that, he'd have a pocket full of spending change by day's end, I thought. I wanted to talk to him about that but didn't get the chance before I heard the voice say, "Train to Savannah, arriving track number two."

After all the white folks got on the train, me and the three other colored folks got on. It was a long walk to where we got on, and there was no one there to help us with our bags either. I took a seat at a window and looked out as we left the station: there was that colored man putting down some bags and a white man giving him a coin. I only wish I could have found out more about that job, I thought as the train moved farther and farther away from the station and from my home.

The ride took a few hours. At one point a colored man came into the train car that held us colored folk. He was dressed in a dark suit, somewhat like the colored man at the station. He also had a funny-shaped hat with a long piece coming out that was shiny. He asked us for our tickets and punched a hole in them and put them on the seat behind us. He, too, had a big smile, kinda like he was glad to see us. I asked what it was that he did, and I asked about what the colored man at the station did. All he said was it was the sweetest work he ever had. He called himself and the other man a "porter."

It was nice talking to the man 'bout trains and stuff. It also made the trip go a bit faster. Before one in the afternoon, we were pulling into the station in Savannah. I watched: there was another colored man, a porter, helping the white folks wit' their bags, and the white folks were pulling change outta their pockets and giving it to the colored man.

After the white folks left the train, we were told that we could leave. I looked around for where the colored folk that were in the train with me was going; there were signs around, but I couldn't read, so there didn't really mean much to me. After a short walk, there was a bench with a bit of roof over it where the colored people stopped to sit. One quickly got up when a woman and a man came toward her. The other sat down, so I did the same. A little while later, two men came toward the bench and the colored man got up and walked over to then.

Fo' a while I was sitting on the bench by myself. A few people walked by me and went around the small building, to where I didn't know. Then there came a chubby man. He was coming toward me at a hurried pace. For the first time since my journey began, I became frightened. Here was this chubby white man coming toward me, and even though he was smiling, I could not find a reason to think this was a good thing.

The man came right up to the bench. Still smiling, he said, "You must be young Cleveland? I'm sorry to get here late, but I had a bit of business to take care of that took much longer than I had hoped it would. I finally made it, and I'm glad to meet you."

I was confused. What was this white man doing knowing my name and even explaining to me that he was late? Who was this person? I wondered.

"I'm here to pick you up," the white man said. "My name is William Brown; I'm a friend of your papa Philip. Come along—we've got a bit of a ways to go and a short time to get there. I've gotta get you settled in," he continued, "and tomorrow we'll have us a good talk so I can figure out how best to help you."

I was still planted in my seat not really knowing just what to do when the man waved me on. I got up, still confused but following the man as he ordered. After we turned the corner of the building, there was the motorcar I had seen Johnnie driving. The white man climbed into the front seat and waved me over to the other side. I hadn't been in Savannah but a short time, and already I was riding with a white man in a motorcar. Maybe things are gonna be OK in this new place, I thought as we rode down the paved roadway.

Riding in a motorcar was different, but if I had to compare it to riding in a wagon, I think I'd prefer the wagon. Heck, I almost fell outta that thing two times when we hit a bump in the road. The seats were soft and nice, but that was really all that I liked about it. After a while we pulled up to a house in the city. There were so many houses close up on each other; I had never seen anything like that before. I had seen stores all grouped together but not houses.

Mr. Brown climbed down from the motorcar after turning off the noise and went to the door of one of the houses. I was told by Mr. Brown to stay in the car until he called for me to come over. He knocked on the door until it opened, and I could see a little colored woman standing at the exit. Mr. Brown spoke with the woman for a bit before he turned to me and waved for me to come over.

I grabbed my bag and made my way to the opened door. "This is young Cleveland Golden," he said to the woman, "and Cleveland, this is Ms. Emma Jackson." I didn't know what to do, so I just nodded my head toward the woman. "You're going to be staying here for a bit or until you can get your bearings in this town," Mr. Brown continued. "I'll be by in the morning to have that chat with you. Until then, I bid you both a good evening." He made his way back to the motorcar.

"Young Cleveland Golden, come on in," the woman said. "You must be hungry. I'll take you to the kitchen, and we can see bout getting you some food in ya." She led the way down a long hallway.

She was right, I had held on to a ham sandwich because I didn't know when it would be before I got to a real meal. Ms. Emma directed me to a chair at a large table the size of which I had never seen before: a whole heap of people could sit at this table and have a meal, I thought. There were some pots and pans on the large stove, and Ms. Emma took down a plate from a cabinet and began to pile food onto it. She glanced back at me and added a bit more to the plate. When she brought to the table, I could see the meal was collard greens, macaroni and cheese, rice with gravy, fried chicken, and some corn bread.

Before I could begin to eat, she showed me to a corner in the large room where there was a pail of water and a washcloth. "You can wash up over there," she said. I quickly got up and made my way to the water and pail, wanting to hurry back to the table and the food that was waiting for me.

Ms. Emma sat at the other end of the table as I ate. Twice she informed me that I didn't have to rush it down and that there was plenty more if I wanted seconds. I was just hungry, and the food was so good that I couldn't stop pushing it down. After I had cleaned the plate, Ms. Emma asked if I wanted more, to which I quickly answered no, feeling that I would bust if I ate another bite. Then she offered me a slice of apple pie. I couldn't say no to that. Now my meal is complete, I thought, as the day's journey began to take its toll on me.

Ms. Emma asked if I were tired, and at that point, I surely was. She asked me to follow her again. This time it was to a staircase leading up. I had never been in a house that had such a thing, but I had no problem following her. At the top of the stairs were many doors, all closed except for one. She led the way to the one door that was open and summoned me into the room. There was a bed fully made up, a dresser with drawers, and an oil lamp burning.

"This is your room, young Cleveland Golden," she said. "I hope it's to your liking."

"It's very nice," I said quickly, noting that the bed was the center of my attention at that time. Maybe tomorrow I'd take a better look around, but for now this was a perfect place to lay my head and get some sleep.

"Good night, young Cleveland Golden," Ms. Emma said as she left the room.

"Good night," I said while making my way to the bed. I dropped my bag on the floor at the foot of the bed and got undressed. I lay down on the firm bed and feel asleep.

"Young Cleveland Golden," someone said after knocking on the door. It was the voice of a man, and I didn't know how to reply. "It's time for breakfast."

"Yes sir," I said after sitting up on the bed. "I'll be there directly."

I looked around the room in an attempt to become familiar with my surroundings. I could not see the amount of sunlight due to the shutters on the window, so I had no idea of what time in the morning it was. I did see a pitcher and a pan on a small table in one corner of the room. I got up and walked over to that area. The pitcher was filled with water, and the pan had a washcloth in it. There was also some brown soap near the pan, so I washed up and got dressed.

Again, there was a knock on the door. This time the voice sounded familiar: it was Ms. Emma. Are you awake, young Cleveland Golden?" she asked.

"Yes," I answered as I opened the door.

"Well, good morning ta ya, young Cleveland Golden," she said with a wide smile. "How'd you sleep?"

"Quite nicely," I replied. I don't know iffin I've ever been in such a nice bed as dis before. Maybe before I could reckon anything I did, but I sho don't ever remember."

"Well, I'm glad you had a good sleep," Ms. Emma said as she led me back down the stairs and to the kitchen with the large table. This time there were other people there. They were sitting all around the table. Ms. Emma pointed me to a seat on the other side of the table where an older man was seated.

"We been waiting for you, young Cleveland Golden," the man said. It was the same voice I heard through the door earlier. "Have a seat, and we can get started with grace."

Everyone bowed their heads.

"Dear Lord God, we are thankful fo' all yo' blessings, we are thankful for yo' grace and yo' mercy, we are thankful fo' this new day you have brought us to, and Lord God, we are thankful that you have given young Cleveland Golden safe passage to our humble home. God, continue to lift him up as you show him the ways you have before him, and bless this place and the food we are about to eat. Amen."

Everyone at the table said amen. I didn't know what to say, so I said amen too as I wiped the tear from my eye. The table became lively as the food was passed from person to person. There were hotcakes and molasses, eggs and bacon, and 'tatas cooked a way I had never seen befo' wit' peppers and onions—this was a great meal.

After breakfast the three women got up and began to clear the table. One of the women was about my age, I reckoned. She had her hair tied with a cloth, but I could see that it was fine and a bit shiny. I wondered for a moment what it would look like without the cloth. I also noticed the sway of her hips as the passed the table going toward the large pan where the dishes were being put. She was pretty too—I sure couldn't miss that about her.

"Young Cleveland Golden," Ms. Emma said in a somewhat louder voice than she had used in the past, which made it get my attention, "Mr. Brown will be coming by to see you shortly, so I 'spect you best be getting ready."

"Yes ma'am," I said and got up from the table. I had to think about that tone of voice Ms. Emma had and wondered if I might have done something wrong; I surely didn't want to offend her in any way. On the way to my room, I realized that I had been staring at the woman who was about my age when Ms. Emma called out to me in that voice I had never heard before. That was probably the problem, but I had to find out if that made Ms. Emma upset with me and why. I'll ask the older man when I get the chance, I thought.

There was not much to do in my room. I made the bed and put my things away in the set of drawers beneath the mirror. Then there was a knock on the door; it was the older man who I sat next to at the table. I opened the door and asked him in. There were a few things I wanted to know from him: I wanted to know where the outhouse was since I didn't know how much longer I could hold my pee, so I asked that first.

"The second door on the left, down the hall," he said. I must have looked confused, so he decided to walk me to the small room. "Just pull this when you're done," he said, showing me a wooden thing hanging on a chain.

I thanked him and closed the door; I was just in time.

When I came out of the small room, the man was still standing in the hallway. I went into the room, and he followed me. I wasn't sure how to begin asking the things I wanted to know and was pleased when he began to talk first.

"My name is Harold Jackson," he said, and Emma is my wife. Mary is our daughter; I'm pretty sure you noticed her," he continued. "She is sixteen and kinda big for her age. At lunch I'll introduce you to the other guests we have staying here. We were getting off to a late start this morning, so I didn't get to properly get you aquatinted with them: some had things to do, and I didn't want to hold them up any longer that I had to. Now was there something else you wanted to ask me?"

"I think I know what I did, and I won't do it again," I said. "You can tell Mrs. Emma that fo' me. I will surely not do that again."

"I was a young man too," Mr. Jackson said, "and I understand how a thing like that could happen."

"I understand, sir," I said.

Mr. Jackson left the room, and I felt really bad. I wasn't sure how it was going to be when I came face-to-face with Mrs. Jackson. Nor did I know if Mary had seen me looking at her that way and what would she think of me. How I felt was not good at all, and I didn't know what to do to fix it. Heck, here I am in the big city fo' one day, and I already done messed up, I thought.

As I sat on the bed feeling as low as could be there was a knock on the door. I began to make my way to open it, and the voice called out, "Mr. Brown is downstairs waiting for you, young Cleveland Golden."

I knew that voice; it was Mrs. Jackson, and she didn't have the same tone of being upset with me that she did after breakfast. I wasn't sure if that was a good or a bad thing, but I knew it was a better tone than before. "Thank you, Mrs. Jackson," I said as I opened the door. I was glad to see that she had a big smile on her face. Maybe she's not upset with me now, I thought.

I closed the door and followed her down the stairs. As we reached the bottom, Mary was coming toward us. I nodded my head and looked away. I noticed that Mrs. Jackson was looking at me. She pointed to the room down the hall and told me that Mr. Brown was in there; she still had a smile on her face.

I followed her instructions. In the large room, there was Mr. Brown. He was dressed nicely in a tan suit with dark-brown boots. I don't remember when I had seen such a fine suit of clothes, and the boots had nary a speck of dirt on them. He was seated on a large chair with padding all over it.

"Come sit down, he said. "We've got to figure out just what you might want to be doing with yourself. Tell me, what kind of work have you done?"

"I'm a farmer," I said proudly, "and a darn good one at that. Heck, I once planted and harvested fourteen acres all by myself. I had melons, and corn and peas, and even a mess of strawberries. I got them in the ground and outta the ground all by myself. That's what I do, and that's what I know."

Mr. Brown looked at me all the while I was talking, but he didn't seem as happy as I thought he should have been. "Is there something wrong?" I asked.

"Well, young Cleveland Golden, there just isn't much use for a farmer 'round here, no matter how good he is," Mr. Brown said. "I might be able to get you some work in one of the plants around town; I'll call in a few favors and see what I can do. Meanwhile, you just sit tight, and I'll get back to you as soon as I find something. By the way, can you read?"

"No sir, I can't," I answered.

"That probably won't be a problem," he said. "You can follow instructions well enough, I'm sure."

"Yes sir, I can," I said as Mr. Brown got up from the large chair with padding.

"I'll be in touch soon," he said and left the room.

Days went by, and I didn't hear from Mr. Brown. My worry was that I wouldn't be able to pay fo' my keep iffin I didn't get me some kind of work. I still had the money I left home with, and I figured that would hold me fo' a little while, but I needed some work. I decided to take a walk round and see if maybe there was someone who might need a fix-it man or somebody to clean up.

As I was walking and looking in the windows, I realized that even if there was a sign saying help needed, I wouldn't even know, and I'd Walk right past it. The next time I come a looking, I better bring somebody along that can read the signs, I thought. Just as I was turning to head back to the house, a man bumped me real hard. He quickly said he was sorry and began to hurry off down the street. I remembered what Papa had said 'bout people doing that and picking yo' pocket. I kept my eye on the man as I checked my pockets; the money I had tied in the cloth in my front pocket was still there, but the dollar bill I had in my hanky was gone. I followed the man, and as he turned the corner, I ran to catch up with him. He looked up at me as I hit him 'side his head, and as he fell down to the ground, I could see my hanky in his hand. I leaned over to take my hanky with the dollar bill, and the man cowered as if he thought I was going to hit him again.

"Don't hit me no mo'," the man said as I opened the hanky to see my dollar was still there.

"I ain't gonna hit you no mo' since I did get my dollar back," I said as I reached down to help him up.

The man looked at me in wonder; I reckon he just didn't know what to think at that time.

"My name Cleveland," I said. "What be yo' name?" I asked as I sized him up and realized that he couldn't have been much older than me.

"I'm William Randall Cook; that be who I is. But my friends they calls me Willy, and I'm hoping you be's a friend," he said with a big smile on his face.

"You just picked my pocket, and you want me to be yo' friend," I said, knowing that I really did want that. "Look, no mo' pickpocketing, especially if you're 'round me," I added, looking Willy straight in the eyes. "Do you think you can do that?

"I sho can, he answered, "and as you can see, I sho ain't good at it anyhow."

"Can you read?" I asked.

"I sho can. Been as far as the seventh grade before I had to drop out to help Mama since Daddy died."

"Oh, yo' papa dead?" I asked.

"Yeah, been dead two years now."

"Is this what you call work?" I asked.

"No, I just saw you looking 'round like you didn't know yo' way, so I decided to try you, kinda see if I could do it. You were my first try, and it damn near got me killed. I ain't fidin' to try that no mo."

I wanted to laugh but thought it better to keep a straight face. "Yeah, if I had had mo' than a dollar in that pocket, I just might have killed you fo' taking it," I said.

"Well, I'm glad it was only a dollar too," Willy said, and we both laughed.

Willy and I walked up and down the streets, him reading what the signs said, even though none said they were hiring. "Since you're not a good pickpocket, what is it that you do to help yo' mama?" I asked.

"I do's odd jobs round town. Today there just wasn't any work available fo' me, so I was on my way to check the stables when I saw you walking 'round looking out of place. Sometime' I can clean up 'round there and pick up some loose change. Wanna walk over there, and see?" Willy said.

I thought about what the stable on Papa's farm was like on cleanup day and how messy that could be. "Maybe tomorrow," I said, not wanting to go back to the house smelling like horse mess.

"OK," Willy said. "Should I meet you here, then?"

I thought about whether to tell him where I was staying and decided not to just yet. "Yep, I'll meet you here tomorrow," I said, realizing that he never did ask me where I was staying.

"Good, Cleveland," he said as he turned to walk away. "Oh, about this same time?" he asked.

"Yeah, this same time," I said, looking to see where the sun was in the sky.

I made my way back to the house and could see Mary in the side yard; she was picking something from the garden. I wanted to go over and help her since the basket she had was almost as big as she was, but I thought about Mrs. Jackson's tone with me the other night. I went in the house and began climbing the stairs; I just wanted to rest fo' a while before dinner time. I was halfway up when Mrs. Jackson called out to me.

"How was yo' day?" she asked in her calm, gentle voice.

"It was just fine," I answered. "Just walked 'round town, kinda getting to know where things are and all."

"Good," she said. "Oh, can you do something fo' me 'fo' you go?"

"Yes'm," I said. What can I do fo' ya?"

"Marys in the yard, and I know she's gonna make that basket she has so heavy. Could you go out and give her a hand?" she said. "I'd surely appreciate it."

"Sure, Mrs. Jackson. I'll do that right now," I replied and turned to walk back down the stairs.

As I began to walk over to where Mary was standing, I decided to clear my throat so as not to frighten her. She turned quickly and asked me, "What are you doing out here?"

"I came to give you a hand with that large basket you have there," I said.

"I really don't need any help," she said while handing me the basket, "but since you're here, you can hold this while I pick a few more plums."

"Whatever you say, Ms. Mary," I said, wanting it to sound as if she was in control of what was going on in her garden.

"Will you be helping me whenever I come out to pick fruit?" she asked.

"Only if you like and yo' mama tells me to," I said.

"So this wasn't your idea," she said.

"I did see you from outside of the house and I did want to come over to help you, but I don't think I would have without yo' mama's consent."

"Is you 'fraid of my mama?" she asked.

"Yes I is," I said. "I don't want yo' mama ever mad at me fo' thinking that I'm outta line with you in any way."

"Suppose I wanted you to get outta line with me?" she asked.

"Well, in that case I'd still look fo' yo' mama's consent, and I know I wouldn't get it, so you'll have to do this on yo' own," I answered, wanting this whole thing to end quickly, feeling that the longer we stayed in this garden, the likelier I would get in trouble with Mrs. Jackson. "Are you 'bout done yet? I asked. "I really need to get to my room befo' dinnertime."

"I reckon I'm done, you're a scaredy-cat," she said with a big grin on her face.

I knew that this was not the end of whatever it was she wanted from me and that I had better stay as far away from her as I possibly could or there was going to be trouble.

As we turned toward the house, I could see Mrs. Jackson looking at us through the window. I was glad that I had kept my distance and didn't give in to flirting with Mary, even though I would have wanted to, seeing how pretty she was and all.

I got to the door, and as it swung open, I searched Mrs. Jackson's face fo' any sign of anger; I was relieved to see that there was none. Her big smile was a welcoming sight.

"Where would you like these?" I asked, wanting very much to get the weight of the basket off my arms.

"You can place it on the table," she said, pointing toward the dining room area, "and thank you."

I went to the dining room and placed the heavy basket on the table, then continued to the stairs leading up to my room. I was glad that I had made it through that and didn't want to go through it again.

All through dinner I could feel Mary's eyes on me; I tried as hard as I could to avoid looking in her direction. I wondered if this was going to become what I'd have to go through every day that I stayed in this house, and that reminded me that I had to get some work so that I could pay my way. After dinner I needed to talk with Mrs. Jackson and find out how much I owed her fo' my stay. But fo' now I just need to keep my eyes offa Mary and keep the peace with this family and me, I thought.

After dinner the women got up and cleared the table, as was always the case. The men sat around fo' a few minutes. I wanted to talk with Mrs. Jackson but wasn't sure if I could with the way things were going. I wondered if I could talk to Mr. Jackson and get the same information; after all, they were married. I decided to give it a try. When the other men were leaving the table, I asked if I could speak with him; he quickly said I could. We walked into the living room area and sat down on the big chair with the padding.

"Mr. Jackson, I need to know how much it's gonna cost me to stay here fo' a while and when is it that I needs to pay up," I said.

"Young Cleveland Golden, yo' gonna have to take that up wit' Emma," he said. "She the one that all arrangements were made wit', and she got all the information. Do you want me to get her now so you can find out what you needs to know 'bout this?"

I stood still fo' a moment, not really sho if I wanted to speak with her at all but knowing that it had to be done at some time so it might as well be right now. "Yes sir," I answered.

Mr. Jackson called, and Mrs. Jackson came into the room. "Cleveland wants ta ask you something," he said.

"OK, what's on yo' mind, young Cleveland Golden?" she said. "You did seem to be a bit on the quiet side at dinner."

"Oh, I was just wondering what I needed fo' my keep here is all. I reckon there is near time fo' me to pay fo' my room and board, and I just needed to know how much."

"You need not worry 'bout that, young Cleveland Golden: yo' room and board has been paid fo' the next two months, and mo' money is there in case you need to stay here longer than that. Yo' daddy done took care of that fo' you, so's you don't have that to worry 'bout. You just concentrate on what it is that you wanna do wit' yo'self, and if you decide you can leave here afo' that time, I will have some money fo' you to help get you started wherever you go. Is that all, young Cleveland Golden?" she asked. "I needs to straighten out my kitchen."

"Yes'm," I said, not knowing what to say after hearing that Papa had done so much to see to it that I got a good start.

I walked to the stairs. I couldn't stop the tears from streaming down my face. I'll make him proud is what I'll do; I'll make him proud, I thought.

It was hard fo' me to sleep. I couldn't stop thinking of what Papa had done.

The next morning, I could see the sunlight coming through the shutters, but I didn't want to get up. I knew it was early that the knock came on the door. It was Mrs. Jackson. "Young Cleveland Golden," she said in her soft voice, "there is someone here to see you."

"OK, Mrs. Jackson," I answered. "I'll be right down."

I thought for a moment, then figured that it must be Mr. Brown. He had probably found some work fo' me. I went to the basin and poured some water in it, enough to wash my face, before I went down to see Mr. Brown. I thought, it's early, so I just may need to go to work right away. Yep, that's probably it: he's here to tell me that he found me a job and I need to get right over to it.

I rushed to get dressed; if I had to leave right away, I would be ready. When I reached the bottom of the stairs, I could hear a familiar voice coming from the living room—it was Johnnie. I'd know that voice anywhere. I had heard it all throughout my life. I ran the rest of the way; I couldn't wait to see his face.

I rushed to greet him, and he reached out his arms. I hugged him as if I hadn't seen him in years. It really wasn't that long ago he came to visit Papa and the rest of us on the farm, but it was just so good to see him. He was family.

After the hugs we sat on the large chair with the padding. He was dressed in fine clothes and seemed taller than when I had last seen him. I finally realized that he seemed taller because he was wearing boots for shoes. We talked fo' what seemed like hours before he got up to leave.

"I want you to have a key to my place," he said. "In case you ever need to come there, you will be able to get in. I don't live too far from here, and I have this paper with the address on it. You can ask someone where it is and come by anytime." He handed me the key and the paper with the writing on it.

I put the items in my front pocket where I kept the hanky with the money Papa gave me. We hugged again, and Johnnie left the house. I didn't see which way he went. I really didn't want him to leave, so I never left the large room. After a while I returned to my room. I had told Johnnie what Papa had done fo' me by paying my way and giving my all this time to find my way without worry. He told me that Papa had done the same fo' him when he left home. He said that Papa was good that way and that someday we should think about giving back to him what he spent on us. I didn't have to think about it fo' mo' that a minute befo' agreeing that it was a good idea to do that.

The next day I had planned to go out with Willy again; we had been making a little change working in the stables. Before I was ready to leave the house, Mr. Brown came by. He seemed so excited, and as we sat to talk, I waited eagerly to hear what he had to say.

"I found something I think you might like," he said, still wearing a big grin on his face. "I found you a job you can start as soon as tomorrow."

I was still waiting for him to tell me what the job was. The only thing I would have really liked was a chance to work on a farm; that I knew I would like. I was not so sure about anything he might have come up with, but I did need a job. I need to be able to get out of this house before something happens with Mary, who has become more brazen lately, I thought.

"What is it?" I asked, not wanting to wait any longer. "Could you please tell me what the job is and where it is, Mr. Brown, sir?" I asked again.

"Oh, it's stocking and unloading for Mr. Samuels at his trading store. You will also have to clean up: you sweep and mop up from time to time," he said.

I was not so sure how I felt about that, but I did know where it was; Willy and I would look into the window at the white folks as they went in and did their business.

"I have the address for you," Mr. Brown said as he reached for a piece of paper in his jacket pocket.

"I know where it is," I said. "I been over thataway a few times afo' so I can get there, but I don't think that he lets colored people in there, do he?"

"No, don't you go waking into the front door; that is not allowed," Mr. Brown said. "You can go around the back where there is another door. Go to that door and knock twice—don't knock more than that and wait for someone to open the door. That's how you will report to work every day. Got it? Never go to the front door, ever."

Mr. Brown left after telling me to be there at nine in the morning. I couldn't wait to tell Willy that I finally had a regular job. Willy was turning into a pretty good friend, even though some of his advice was not something that I wanted to follow, such as having sex with Mary if she really wanted me to. I thought, Mary is a flirt and would only cause me problems if I were to do anything with her. Even though I find her good to look at and she is built like a prefect woman, my gut tells me to stay away, and that's what I'ma do.

Willy and I hung around for most of the day. We even walked around to see where the second door to the trading store was. He was happy fo' me that I got a real job. He was planning on trying to get into the box company at the end of town. He heard that there were some openings there and was gonna ask me if I wanted to go to, but now that I had a job, we'd just have to figure out when we would have time to get together and do stuff as friends. I was hoping that he would get a job, too, so we could do more things—he said that there was a place where they had dancing and live music bands and stuff. I had never been to anything like that and wanted to go just to see what it was like fo' myself. I didn't know much about dancing, but I heard that some of us colored folk have a natural knack fo' that kinda thing.

Willy and I parted a bit early fo' us, but I wanted to back to the house and tell Mr. and Mrs. Jackson 'bout my job. I also wanted them to help me to get up in time so's I would not be late on the first day of work.

When I got to the house, I saw Mary and Mrs. Jackson in the hallway. "Good afternoon, Mrs. Jackson. Good afternoon, Mary," I said as I approached the both of them.

"Good afternoon, young Cleveland Golden," Mrs. Jackson said. Mary just gave me a sexy look. "I hears you got yo'self a job. I reckon you be leaving soon. Be nice iffin you let me know 'fo' you go."

"I am not leaving right away iffin that's OK with you," I said. "I think I'll need some time to get myself together first." I could see the smile on Mary's face. She still has time to mess with me, I thought.

"Yo' welcome to stay as long as you like," Mrs. Jackson said. All I need you to do is just let me know when you decide it is yo' time to go. Now go and get ready fo' dinner, and I'll let someone know to call in the morning so you can eat and make it to work on time. Go on and get ready."

I turned and walked toward the stairs. Mary walked in front of me, making sure that I could see her behind shaking as she walked. I still had to be careful 'round Mary 'cause she was surely thinking that her time was running out, and my sense was that she did not like the part of not getting everything that she wanted so I knew she was gonna come at me wit' everything she had.

Dinner was nice, even though Mary gave me the eye all through it and I wondered if Mr. and Mrs. Jackson were seeing the same thing that I was seeing. Maybe I should really think about leaving this house sooner rather than later, I thought. I will begin looking around after work, and there is always Johnnie's if things get too out of hand fo' me to handle round here.

I hurried back upstairs after dinner; I wanted the safety of my room. Mr. Brown had told me that there was a good bit of toting and cleaning in this job, so dress was not an issue. I laid out some pants and a shirt so I could get dressed quickly in the morning. I didn't find out who was going to wake me in case I was not up, but I was pretty sure that somebody would and that was all that mattered. This whole thing was so new to me; I had never really worked fo' anybody other than papa, sep fo' the times I did some picking at the Jones farm to help.

The door opened slowly. I could see the slender leg of a woman; it was Mary. She had a cloth wrapped round her, which dropped to the floor as she came closer to my bed. I could see her firm breasts and slender figure. As she climbed onto the bed, I could see that she was totally naked. I felt paralyzed as she climbed under the covers and on top of me. She took my hand and placed it on her breast; I wanted to pull away but could not move. I knew that this was leading to that very thing I didn't want to happen. I began to cry out. "No, no, stop," I screamed.

I leaped up in the bed. It was a dream. I had been dreaming, but it seemed so real. I was sweating, as if I had worked six acres in the hot sun fo' a whole day. I didn't know if I'd be able to sleep again. The bed was wet from my sweating. I found a dry spot and lay there hoping that sleep would come I had a big day ahead of me tomorrow, and I needed the rest. Before long I felt sleep coming on.

I awoke as I heard the knock on the door. The voice was soft in tone; I knew it was Mrs. Jackson. I looked toward the window. The sun was not yet as high as I was used to seeing it when I got up. I was sure it was much earlier, but I did remember Mrs. Jackson saying that I would have breakfast before going to work. That would explain why it was so early.

"I'm up," I shouted toward the closed door. "Thank you."

"OK," Mrs. Jackson said. "I'll be in the kitchen. Just come on down so's you can eat something before you go."

"OK," I answered, "I'll be there directly. It sho is nice of you to get up so early to get me on my way," I added, but there was no answer from Mrs. Jackson.

It took me a short while to use the bathroom and wash up and get dressed before I made my way down to the kitchen. To my surprise, there was two other house guests sitting at the table.

"Good morning," I said as I took my seat.

One of the guests said grace, and Mrs. Jackson brought the food to the table. It was a typical breakfast with all the trimmings: eggs, bacon, grits, and pan bread. It seeded in my mind that I wasn't the only one who got up to go to work. I laughed at myself fo' thinking that it was only me.

It was a short walk to the trading store. I wasn't sure of the time, so I made sure to hurry. I walked the back door and knocked two times as I was told by Mr. Brown to do, then I waited. No one came to the door, and I thought about knocking again but I could hear Mr. Brown saying don't knock again so I looked round fo' a place to sit as I waited fo' Mr. Samuels to open the door. Just as I sat on an old log, the door opened.

"Boy, why didn't you knock on the door?" the man said in an angry voice. "I've been waiting for you for ten minutes, which is gonna be taken out of your pay," the tall white man continued. "Now bring your black ass in here so I can show you what I need you to do."

I wanted to tell him that I had been there for some time, and I did knock on the door, but something inside of me said that I had best not say anything, so I followed him into the store.

The man took me to a side room where there was sacks piled on the floor. He pointed to the sacks and told me to carry each one from where they were on the floor to another room and to place them on the shelves, he pointed out to me. "When you finish doing that, sweep the floor where the sacks where at," he said. "That should keep you busy for a while. I'll check back on you in a few hours."

He walked out of the room after giving me that look, I remembered white folks had when I was a boy and me and Papa went to town to sell our crops to the stores. I began to carry the sacks from one room into the other; getting it done quickly, I swept the floor and put the trash in a bin. I looked around for something else to do, not knowing when this man was gonna come back in the room and surely knowing that I wasn't going to look for him. I noticed that the items in the room where I put the sacks where not neatly stacked, so I just made sure that they were placed so that they could be seen easily. When I was almost finished with that, the tall white man came back into the room.

"I see you're not as lazy as that other nigger I had in here before," the man said. "We might just get along. Now go outside and clean up that back area; there's gonna be a delivery here a little later. Go on, get," he added while looking at the work I had done with the things on the shelf. "Looks pretty good."

I looked round the back area, searching fo' where things were and where things might go. When I figured things out, I began the clean up. I decided not to make this happen too fast. He just might have me rebuild the whole store if he can't find something else fo' me to do, I thought. By the time the wagon came 'round the back, I had finished cleaning the entire area.

The tall white man came outta the store and quickly looked round the area. I could see by the look on his face that he was pleased with the work I had done. "Boy, come help unload this stuff off the wagon," he called to me.

I quickly responded and waited fo' instructions on just what he wanted me to do.

"Take these boxes and put them in the room that the sacks were in," he said. "Just place them on the floor, then take the sacks of flour and put them next to the sacks on the shelf in the other room."

I didn't say a word as I lifted the boxes and made my way to the room. I placed them as told and took the flour to the other room and put it on the shelves. When I was done, I saw that the tall white man was in the other room looking through the boxes. I wasn't sure of what he wanted me to do, so I cleared my throat so as to let him know that I was done.

"You can go have lunch," the tall man said. "I have to make sure that everything I ordered is here." I realized that his voice was different. I wasn't sure of what that meant, and I surely was going to try to find out. "Come back in a hour," he said.

I wasn't much on telling time that away, but I figured that I could probably make it back to the house and see if they were having a meal 'round now, and iffin so, I could eat something there.

CHAPTER 3

I had been working at the trading store some many years and had complete run of the day-to-day things that were going on. I knew all the deliveries and what each one would bring. I had moved outta Mr. and Mrs. Jackson's house over three years ago, although I did stop by from time to time to chat with them. I really couldn't thank them enough for all that they had done fo' me.

Mary was still wild, and I heard that she got herself in a way messing with one of the boarders, who took off after hearing that she was with child. I don't know if the story is true or not, but she did leave town fo' a while and when she came back, she was different. She finally married a fella from 'round here somewhere, and they moved to another state. She came back after a while.

Mr. Samuels and I were getting along fairly well. He felt that he needed to call me a nigger from time to time; I was pretty much used to it, and it didn't really mean a whole lot to me sepin when he decided to do it in front of other white folk. Later on, he'd say he didn't mean much by that and I'd just nod my head. It seemed to me that white folks had shown out like that to other white folks, just to show who was in charge. Really, I wondered what he was gonna do when I told him that I'd be leaving there soon to go and work fo' the box company. Willy done been there all this time and worked his way up, so he was telling me to come there where I'd make mo' money and have better hours. As it was, I didn't have no mo' money than the day I first walked in the back door of Mr. Samuels, and I didn't reckon he was gonna give me ner penny mo'. I was gonna tell him after I checked in the deliveries fo' today and placed them away. Then he'd know that I'd be leaving working there after next week, so he needed to find somebody else fo' this job.

The day at work was going well until a white woman came in complaining 'bout something; whatever it was, it really made Mr. Samuels quite mad. Heck, he was cursing and carrying on, not to the white woman but to his self, and after a while, he started out on me. It seemed that something she had brought had weevils in it and worms and stuff, according to her. She said that she was going to tell the townspeople not to buy from him. He said that would hurt his business, and then he began to blame me fo' it. He said that I should have kept the place cleaner, and that kind of thing would not have happened. He began to call me a stupid nigger and said he was gonna take it out of my next week's pay. I said that I wasn't gonna be here fo' that 'cuz I quit.

He looked at me as I began to walk out the door. "Nigger, you better come back here," he said as the door closed behind me. That was the last time I ever saw Mr. Samuels.

I took a week off before I took the job at the Eagle Box Factory. The first thing I noticed was the noise; it must have been the noisiest place on God's green earth.

I was taken to a room where the boxes came down a slide and I had to pile them up. That was it; I just picked them off the slide and put them in a pile. 'Sep fo' the noise, this was not nearly as hard as what I was doing at the trade store, and there was nothing in the boxes, so they were that much easier to carry. The hours were steady too: I was there at nine and left at four. There was a bell to start and a bell to stop. It didn't matter much that I didn't know the time that way—all I needed to know was that the bell rang out.

Willy and I got to go out together on the weekends. My apartment at 110 Walnut Street was a short distance from the factory. Willy and I would meet in the morning; he lived a few blocks away, and we'd go to work together. He'd be outside waiting.

Willy still looked after his mother. I really liked that about him. He was a good-looking man and probably could have got just about any woman he wanted and married up, but he chose to take care of her.

At times I'd think about Mr. Samuels and how he wasn't all that bad. Heck, he did teach me how to drive a motorcar, even though it was so that I could take him and his wife 'round and tote and lift fo' him when they went shopping. Heck, and all these white folk calls me nigger and boy; at lease with him, I was learning things and getting paid to listen to all that. He even gave me time off to go and visit Papa mo' than one time. I hears that he done fired three people since I been gone from there. I ain't been that way to see, but I does hears that.

Willy and I planned to go to the dance joint during the weekend. He said that there was gonna be a band of black folk playing and that they had a woman singer that was really good to listen to. I was kinda looking forward to it since I had been down there a few other times, and I liked the singing and the dancing. Hell, I even did a bit of dancing myself, and I wasn't so bad, the girl I danced with said.

In the time I been at the box factory, they done got me moved 'round to setting up loads fo' the wagons and motorcars to pick up. Doing this also got me mo' money in my pocket, some from the boss (he called it a raise) and some from people after I helped them get the boxes onto their wagons and motorcars. It would only be a few pennies and sometimes they didn't give me nothing, but at the end of the week, it added up.

Saturday rolled 'round, and I was getting ready fo' the night's goings-on. Willy was coming by to pick me up. I wasn't sho iffin we were going to ride with Carl, a friend of Willy's. I tried to like him, but he drank too much and would sometimes cause problems.

I always liked to have a backup plan fo' getting home whenever we went out with that guy. There was a fella that lived just up the road a bit from me, and he would usually be there. I would check with him to ask if I could ride home with him and his wife; so far, they had never said no to me. That way I wouldn't have to put up with Carl when he drank too much and could still keep the peace with Willy since he seemed to like the guy.

When we go to the joint, the place was jumping: the music was a going, and the dance floor was packed like a box full of baby chicks. The woman singer wasn't on the stage yet, so I figured that she hadn't sung yet. Me and Willy found a seat in the back corner off from the bar. Carl headed straight for the bar; he'd have to find us whenever he got a drink.

After a long performance the band stopped, and the sweaty people rushed to find a place to sit. The woman singer was about to come on, I guessed. A good bit of time went by, and there was no woman singer. Finally, the band began to play again. I could tell most of the people there was angry that the woman didn't show. I had never heard her before, so it really didn't matter to me at all. What I liked was the music and the dancing, and that was still going on.

I searched the room fo' the woman I had danced wit' befo' but didn't see her anywhere. I guess I won't be dancing tonight, I thought. Then I saw this woman out the corner of my eye. She seemed to be with two other women. There were no men round them at all, and she was so pretty and dressed to the nines. I wondered what a pretty little woman like her was doing without a man close by to look after her. I wanted to go over and introduce myself even though I kinda felt like I had seen her somewhere before. I surely wasn't going over there with that "Don't I know you from somewhere?" line, but I had to meet her; there was no doubt about that. Well, here goes, I thought.

"Good evening, ladies," I said, looking directly at her. "Would you like to dance?" I extended my hand to her.

My heart was pounding as I wondered if she was just gonna say no and turn away.

"Yes," she said while putting her hand in mind.

I helped her up, and we made our way to the dance floor.

"My name is Cleveland," I said, almost in her ear, while the slow music played.

"My name is Hattie," she answered in a soft, well-spoken voice. "It's nice to finally meet you," she continued. "I've seen you around town and in Elly's place from time to time. Usually eating by yourself."

"I knew that I had seen you 'round but just wasn't sho of where, so I didn't want to come to you with that," I said. "Do you come here much?" I asked, realizing that I didn't remember seeing her the times I had been there before.

"No, I don't," she answered quickly as if she didn't want me to think that she was the type of woman who had nothing to do but hang out in places like this. "My friend Eva Mae asked me to accompany her here tonight, and I had the day off, so I came here with her."

"Oh, I myself don't come out here much; this is only the third time fo' me," I said. "I do like the music, and I like to dance. I'm from a small town, and we don't have this kind of place to go to, or at least I never been to anything like this sep since I came here. I 'spect a country boy like me would be excited by all the goings on in a place like this."

"Well, how'd you get to be such a good dancer?" she asked.

"I don't know how good a dancer I am and if I tell you, I know that you're gonna laugh, but I just watched everybody else, and when I got home, I danced with myself.

"I would get out one of my shirts and pretend it was a woman and dance in front of the looking glass. I really never tried it out before today, so you're actually my very first dance partner. It seems like you completed my lesson; hats off to you, Ms. Hattie." I could see the smile on her face after I said that.

"Well, you studied you dance moves very well, Mr. Cleveland," she said. "I'm glad to have been you test run," she continued as the music stopped. "I hope we get to do this again sometime."

I walked her back to her seat. I pulled out the chair for her to sit down and announced, "I'm returning this lovely woman back to your care. Be sure to look after her for me." Then I turned and walked away. I looked back to see if she was looking my way, and she was.

When I returned to my table, Carl was there with a tall glass of white whiskey, and he was already slurring his speech. Willy was listening to whatever it was that Carl was trying to say. I was on top of the world.

"How'd it go?" Willy asked as he looked me in the eye.

"She is the one," I answered as I turned round to where she was seated. My expression quickly changed as I noticed that neither she nor her friend Eva Mae was at the table. I searched the dance floor, hoping to not see her with someone else holding her, and did not see her anywhere. My night was over; all I wanted to do was find her. I wondered if this was some kind of dream, if there really wasn't a Hattie and I hadn't just met the woman of my dreams and I was gonna wake up and find none of this had really happened at all. Just like after that dream I had back when I was living in the boarding house, when I thought that Mary had come into my bed and was trying to get with me, I felt sick. I wanted to go out and look for Hattie. Heck, I didn't even ask her where she lived, I thought. I may never see her again.

I went through my mind, searching for hints that might help me find her. Three days had passed since that dance, and all I had was the words in my head: "I've seen you around town and in Elly's place from time to time. Usually eating by yourself." I should have known where she might have seen me 'round town. I didn't really go very far and usually it was with Willy, and she hadn't mentioned him. I went to Elly's place every day hoping that she would show up there and I would find out how to reach her when I wanted to, but she hadn't been there either. I just don't know what to do, I thought. I had already told Willy that we'd be goin' to the dance hall this weekend.

I thought, it's been ten days and nothing. How could someone just drop off the earth like that? I've eaten as much of the outside cooking as I can stand, and going to the dance place means nothing if she's not there. I guess I just better forget about Hattie, even thought I can't seem to get her off my mind. Heck, even Willy is starting not to want to be 'round me 'cause I be moping round like some little child who has lost his best friend to another child.

Weeks went by, and although I did think about her every day, it was becoming a little bit easier with the passing of time. I stopped going to the dance place; it was just too much to bear. Willy didn't push me on it. He and Carl continued to go, and he'd come to me at work with the story of how much trouble Carl had caused after drinking too much. I would laugh and be thankful that I hadn't been a part of that.

It had been a while since I'd gone to Elly's place, so I decided to stop there on the way home. I had been cooking fo' myself but thought I'd give myself a day off. I went to the counter and asked that my dinner be placed in a tote bag so the I could take it home; after paying the eighteen cents, I took a seat to wait fo' my food. I looked round at the tables only to see the same faces.

"Cleveland, your order is ready," the woman called out, and I got up to go to pick it up. That's when I heard that soft voice.

"Been a while. Where have you been keeping yourself?"

I was excited: I knew that voice even though I had only heard it that night on the dance floor. "Hattie," I cried out, "I been looking high and low fo' you. You just was nowhere to be found. It's been weeks. How could you have not been seen 'round town fo' weeks? The whole town ain't but so big, and fo' some reason, I couldn't find you anywhere. How can that be?"

"It is possible if you have a job like I do," she said.

"What kinda job is that where you don't show up anywhere in town fo' weeks at a time?" I asked. "I mean, every job lets you go home fo' a bit."

"Well, not my job," she answered. "I sometimes have to stay at work for long periods of time. I even have living quarters where I work, for those times that I need to stay."

"I never heard of work that would keep you like that, lessin you takes care of white folks' churen and da needs you all the time."

"It's not that, but I am a cook for a family, and as their cook, I sometimes have to stay over, like for times when they have company or if they go away to the other house; when they do, I go with them. I also get paid very well for my work," she said.

"So, how'd you get out now, and fo' how long?" I asked.

"Well, there is nothing going on for the next two days, so I'll make enough food for them, and I get to go home to my place for a day or so."

"I'm not gonna make the same mistake I made before—how can I get in touch with you?" I asked while in my mind I thought there was really no way that I could.

"Well, you could start by walking me home after I pick up some food; I only live a block from here. Then I'll let you know how to figure out when I'm at work or how to get in touch with me."

"I'm fo' that," I said as I waited fo' her to order her food. I reached in my pocket and pulled out the change to pay fo' her meal.

"I can buy my own food," she said as she searched in her bag.

"I know you can," I said, "but it would be my pleasure to do it just this time iffin you don't mind. I really would like to."

"OK," she said, and we sat down and waited fo' her order to be called.

"It took a few minutes before the woman called for Hattie to come get her order. After that we began the walk to her house. It was a lovey night for a walk, before I could begin enjoying just walking and talking with her, we were at the house.

"You sho was right: it ain't but a short walk to yo' place," I said.

"I told you it was just up the way a bit," she said as we arrived at the door. "We can go to the kitchen where you can eat that food while it's still hot," she continued.

She opened the door, which led into a large room that we passed through to get to the kitchen, where there was a small table with two chairs. Hattie pointed to one of the chairs and told me to sit there while she went to the cupboard to get us some plates.

"I could eat right outta the container," I said quickly, not wanting her to make a mess with dishes.

"I'm sure you could," she said with a small smile on her face, "but you don't have to. It's really not a bother, and I will have to clean up my plate anyhow. One more won't make that much of a difference."

"I just don't wanna come to yo' house fo' the very first time and cause you to have ta do extra work on my account," I said. "You just might not wanna have me over again iffin I'm gonna cause you to do that."

Hattie came over to the table with the two plates and sat in the other chair, passing a plate over to me, along with a large spoon. "Just eat," she said.

We sat at the table and had our meals while getting to know each other. We even found humor in learning about each other's background. I reckoned that she had a bit of a time understanding me, and I sho had a time understanding her. It was a good thing that she had some book learning, and she said she understood why I had none at all. She said that she'd help me with things I would need to say better. I said that she was the prettiest teacher I could ever have, and we both laughed. We spent a good bit of time talking and laughing together, but I thought that I had better be getting home and let her get some rest. She had to get up to work tomorrow, and so did I.

"I'll be bidding you good night," I said as I got up from my chair. She didn't say anything, but she did walk me to the door.

"Good night," she said as she opened the door.

"I'd like to call on you again," I said.

"That would be nice," she said. "I will know what my schedule is when I go to the house tomorrow."

"Then I'll come by tomorrow, and you can let me know," I said. "Maybe we can do something this weekend?"

"We'll just wait and see about that," she said with a smile on her face. "Now go."

She had the prettiest smile, I thought. "See you soon," I said as the door closed.

The courtship had been going pretty well until the talk of marriage came up; over time I had asked at least a dozen times. I thought, Heck, I even spent good money on this damned diamond ring. There must be some real reason why she won't marry me. We seems to be getting along all right, or if not, she sho ain't letting on to me that there is something wrong. I's even sat still while she learns me things. I just don't know what else I needs to be doing to make her know that I'll be a good man to her and I ain't afraid of working hard to build her a good life. I even got a better job at a better company so's I could make mo' money to provide fo' her. I'm gonna ask her just one mo' time, and iffin she says no again, I'ma leave her alone and go on my way. That's the way I needs to handle this: just one mo' time, and I'm gone. Heck, I can't do that. I really loves this woman, and what I need to do is ask if there is something that's holding her back from wanting to get married. It just might be something we can fix so's we'd able to at lease plan it fo' another time. No matter what, I'd rather be with her than without her, so whatsinever she wants to do, I'll do. I haven't seen her in three days, and I just can't wait till later on, when I'll be with her again. I've gotta think, too, that this workin' the way she do, not knowing from day to day what or where she is going to be, could be harder for her than she's letting on. That maybe the real question I should be asking her: Is she tired of all the work she has to do fo' that family? Does she want to be home with some churen of her own and not have to work at all? I thinks I could make her a good home without her having to work any mo'. If need be, I can find other work around town to add to the money I make now. I'll check with Willy and see iffin he could find me some extra work somewhere. He always knows stuff like that, even thought I ain't seen much of him when Hattie's around we's still best friends and all.

It was Wednesday, and I had to go home and clean up before going over to visit Hattie fo' dinner. I could see why that family wanted her all the time to cook fo' them 'cause she was the bet cook I'd ever seen; she even beat Mama on most things.

I got home and washed up, put on my Sunday go-to meeting clothes, and headed out the door. I quickly realized that I forgot the ring after getting about two blocks from the house; I turned around and went back to get it. You never know, I thought, tonight just may be the night. I got back to the apartment and went to the drawer where I kept the ring. I picked up the small box, opened it and took a look, snapped the box closed, and put it in my suit pocket. Now I was ready to see Hattie.

The walk seemed to take forever. I was excited about seeing her but not about what might have happened if I did ask her again to marry me. I think I'll just not rush to talk about that and see what she wants to talk about, I thought. I could see from the street that her light was on, so she was home; that brought a smile to my face. I knocked on the door and waited for her to open it fo' me. I had a key, as she had a key to my place, but I never used it when I knew that she was there.

"Hi," I said as I entered the small hallway.

"Hi," she said while looking me over. "You look very nice."

"I just threw on something, hoping to catch your eye," I said.

"Well, you sure did," she said, "but I didn't know we were going out. I did cook all this food, but maybe I better go and get dressed up for dinner. What do you think?"

"No, you look just fine," I said as I leaned in to kiss her.

"Are you sure that I can keep on these rags while you're dressed so fine?" she said.

"You look just fine, and never are you in rags," I said. "Fact is, yo' the best dressed I know."

Dinner went well, with the small talk and all. I enjoyed listening to her, given the way that she spoke her words. I wondered if this would be a good time to ask my question again; after all, we were both in a really good mood. She told me about things that were going on in the big house, and I talked about work. The funny parts were about the white folks, and we both laughed at that.

"You know, I still want you to be my wife," I said, not taking the time to think my way out of saying it.

"I know you think that I'd make you a good wife," she said, "and I probably would, but I know that your love is the land. I've listened to you talking about how you worked the fields, and I could see that it all means a lot to you. It's who you are and what you really love, and I can understand that. I wouldn't want anything other than to see you happy, and you just maybe happy with me in this city setting for a while, but when it really hits you that you are a farmer, the little happiness you thought you could hold on to will not be enough. That's what I'm afraid of: I'm not sure of what will become of us when that day comes. You know what I want is to save up enough money to own my own eatery, either here in this town or up north somewhere. You…well, you want a farm somewhere near where you're from. Those are two different worlds, but if you want, I won't keep letting you down—I care about you too much to do that—and I'll marry you."

It was the first time I was at a loss for words. I reached into my pocket and pulled out the ring as I moved from my seat to where she was sitting. I got on one knee and asked again, "Will you marry me?" as I held the ring in my hand.

"Yes, I will," she answered as she gave me her left hand. I placed the ring on her finger. I was surely the happiest man in the world that day.

We were married six months later. It was a small affair with just family and friends and my good friend Willy, who stood by my side. She had her best friend there, and I was glad that Johnnie was there too. I wanted Papa to come, but it was harvesting time and he could not get away. We planned to visit him as soon as Hattie could get some time off.

The party after jumping the broom went well until Willy's friend had too much to drink and Willy had to leave early to get him home. Willy came back a bit later, and we all had a great time. I looked at the people in my life, and for the very first time, I felt that I had all the right things going on in my life with all the right people there too. I was really happy.

It wasn't mo' than a year befo Hattie gave birth to our son Grover. He was a fat little thing and gave her a run befo' coming on outta her. We were surely scared 'cause there was a heap of screaming and moaning coming from the room that he was being born in. I wanted to try and see if I could do something to help but was told to wait in the other room fo' the arrival.

It must have been the better part of the whole night befo' he finally came; I had fallen asleep and woke up when

I heard the loud crying baby. I rushed into the room to see how Hattie was doing only to find that she was sleep and the woman that had come to help her was holding the baby boy. "It's a boy," she said as she put him in my arms.

That's when I saw just how big he was and cute too. He looked up at me as though he was trying to figure out who I was. "I'm yo' papa," I said, "and you's my little boy. I names yo' Grover Cleveland Golden, my son."

I held on to him until the woman asked me to give him to her so that she could clean him up well afo' waking up Hattie to feed him. I didn't want to let him go.

A year and a half went by before Hattie got some good time off while the family she worked for, the Salases, went away to visit a family member up north. We used this time to go and visit Papa and the family on the farm. I had hoped that after seeing what farm life was really like, Hattie would maybe change her thinking about living on a farm, which was still something I really wanted to do again someday.

We weren't there mo' than a few hours afo' the complaining began. "These bugs and mosquitoes are eating me alive," she said while we sat out on the porch. "I need to go inside with Grover before they eat him too."

I knew then that this was not gonna go as I had wanted it to. This was what we did at the end of a day of farmwork: sit on the porch have a drink and talk. And she couldn't do that.

The visit was not a good sign to me, although I really enjoyed spending some time back in the fields. It was like I had never left. I got to clear four acres and turn the land so that it would be ready fo' some planting in the season to come. Me and papa worked from one end to another, passing each other along the way; it was just like old times. I felt bad that Hattie wasn't having a good visit, but I sho was.

We hardly spoke a word on the trip back home. I was a bit upset because we had to leave early since Hattie was having such a hard time with farm life. Grover was getting the hang of it. He seemed to like the animals. I do believe that the goats were his favorite, and he and the dog got along just great. I did feel sorry fo' Hattie cuz she was getting the bad end of bites from the flies and mosquitos. I wondered iffin it was due to that sweet stuff she'd put on each day. I liked it 'cuz she smelled so good, but it seems that I wasn't the only one—the insects kinda liked it too. At any rate, we were on our way home, and I'd figure out how to get back in her good graces again soon, I hoped.

1916

The year came in, and Hattie was still pregnant. She had thought that she would have had this baby by now, but on January 5, we had our second son. Joseph Herman Golden wasn't as much of a problem coming into the world as Grover had been. At six pounds, eight ounces, he just popped on out. I was there as he did, and the midwife handed him right over to me as she cut the cord to separate him from his mama. Even his cry was a bit different than that of Grover. I checked to see that he had all his toes and fingers as I wiped him off with the damp cloth I was given for that purpose.

I looked over at Hattie, and her arms were stretched out. I wanted to hold on to him a bit longer but thought it wise to hand him over to his mama.

"He's a right good-looking child," I said as I placed him in her arms. I went out into the kitchen and sat at the table. I was happy to have met my new son. I went in the bedroom to check on Grove; if he was still awake, I'd take him to see his brother. What I really wanted was to have a reason to go back in and see the baby again.

Grover was asleep, so I woke him up. "Come and meet your brother," I said to the sleepy child.

We went into the bedroom, and I got to hold Joseph again. "This is your brother," I said, holding the newborn near Grover's face. "Say hello to him."

"Hello," Grover said. "Now can I go back to bed?"

"Go back to bed," Hattie said to the sleepy boy, "and you should not have woken him up," she said to me.

"I just wanted him to meet his brother," I said.

"I know what you wanted," she said with a big smile on her face.

I smiled back as I drew closer to her, giving her a kiss and handing the baby back to her. "I'll be in the other room if you need anything," I said as I left the room.

Two months had gone by, and I was looking forward to taking a trip south to visit Papa and let him see his new grandson. Hattie was not on board with that; she still remembered how hard the farm was on her. I offered to make it a short trip, a few days or so, but she just wasn't giving in.

"It very important to me that Papa gets to see his grandchildren," I said to her.

"I know it is," she said, "but I just don't think that I could stand that right now, and with the baby being so young, I don't want to put him through that at this time."

"He's doing good, and he's so strong. Heck, he eats all the time, so I know he's healthy," I said as I tried to reason with her.

"No, and that's final," she said. "I'm not taking this baby on a train ride or to a farm where the bugs can do him harm; I'm just not doing it."

"Well, can we figure out when you think it would be a good time to visit so's I have something to say to Papa?" I asked.

"I can't even think about that right now," Hattie said as she headed for the door, Joseph in her arm and Grover holding her hand. "I've gotta go." She left the room.

"We'll talk about this later," I said as I heard the front door close. She didn't hear me, I thought, but it isn't over as far as I'm concerned.

I went to work and hardly got anything done; I was just thinking about what I was going to say to Hattie to get her to change her mind. The boss called out to me a few times, telling me to get some work done, but I just couldn't get my mind off my problem. "Go home," the boss, Mr. Smith, said, "since I can't get no work outta you no how, and come back tomorrow with whatever is going on in your mind cleared away."

"Thank you, sir," I said. "I don't mean to be a problem. I just got somethin' on my mind, and I can't seem to shake it loose. I reckon I'll be better by tomorrow, I'm sho."

"Go on," he said. "Just get. 'Fo' other people see you moping round. Get."

"Thank you, sir," I said as I left the building.

On the way home, I picked up a bunch of flowers from the street lady; Hattie always liked it when I brought her flowers. Maybe these will help her to understand my position in this and give in, I thought. I figured that I'd fix dinner also. I knew how tired she was sometimes after cooking fo' that family and having to come home and cook fo' us too.

I thought, I'll look and see what's here and fix her a meal fo' a change. As I opened the icebox where we kept the food, I saw there was two small pots in there; this was usually the case when she had made dinner fo' me as she wasn't coming home that night. I looked into the pots and saw that she had cooked an entire meal. Yes, that meant she was not coming home. I sat at the table trying to remember when she told me she would be working late tonight. I searched through my mind trying to remember. She never did that without telling me days ahead, so she must have told me. Then I remembered three days ago she said that the Salases where having guests and she would probably be better off staying there than trying to come home late at night. I had completely forgotten about that and the suitcase she had when she left. They contained clothes fo' her and the children. Well, we won't be having that talk today, I thought. I brought the pots out and started a fire on the stove. This sho looks good, I thought.

CHAPTER 4

1918

It was near the end of April. The discussions had turned into arguments whenever I mentioned going down to the farm to visit with Papa. I made up my mind that I was going, even if not with Hattie, before June. I thought, If I don't get to take Joseph with me, I can at least tell Papa about him and how big he's getting. He's turning into a cute little curly haired boy.

I had not long been home from work. Hattie was in the kitchen preparing supper when there was a knock on the door. I called out to Hattie that I would get it since I was closer than she was to the door. When I opened it, to my surprise, there was Johnnie. I hadn't seen him since January when he came by to see the baby. I could tell that there was something wrong; Johnnie was always smiling, and now he had this sad look on his face.

"Come on in," I said, holding the door open fo' him. "Can I get you something to eat or drink?"

"Yeah, could you give me a glass of water?" he answered.

I could see Hattie coming into the room. "How are you, Johnnie?" she asked.

"Could you get him a drink of water?" I said to her.

"No, don't leave," Johnnie said. "I can tell you both at the same time. Papa died. I just got the word that he died on the thirtieth of last month."

It was May 3. "And we just getting' to know about this?" I spoke.

"Yeah, they had been trying to reach me and I was outta town fo' a few days. Just got back this morning and just got the news a little while ago."

I couldn't believe it. "Are you sho?" I asked.

"Yeah, I'm sho," Johnnie said with a sternness in his voice. "It seems that he was in the field when he collapsed. One of the farmhands he had working with him was nearby and ran to his aid, but he was dead. Some kind of heart attack or something, they say."

I looked at Johnnie and saw that he had tears in his eyes. I realized that I was crying too. Hattie left the two of us in the room to console each other. When she returned, she had a tray with some glasses on it. She placed the tray on the table and walked back out of the room. I walked over to the cabinet where I kept a bottle of whiskey; I poured Johnnie and me a small drink and handed him the glass. We took a sip of whiskey and sat in silence, each to our own thoughts.

"I'll be able to get down there in a few days," Johnnie said. "They're gonna hold off on the service fo' him until I get there. I know you need some time to get there too."

"I probably will need just a day or so to tell my boss that I need some time off," I answered. "It should not be a problem, but I don't think that I can get Hattie and the kids to go on this little notice. I'll see."

"Hey, why don't you stay and have some dinner with us?" I asked Johnnie. "There's plenty of food, and you know that Hattie is the best cook in town."

"Nah, I think I'm gonna go home and get myself together," Johnnie said just as Hattie was returning to the room.

"Come on, you two," she said. "I fixed you something to eat, and it's on the table."

I looked over at Johnnie, and he looked back at me. "Let's eat," he said.

We didn't speak much during dinner. I was glad that Johnnie had stayed, and by the way he cleaned his plate, I could tell that he needed a good home-cooked meal.

I was on my way back home to South Carolina; Papa's funeral would be in two days. Hattie wasn't with me. It seemed that she was needed at the big house for a big event of some kind. Having talked to her after Johnnie told us about Papa's passing, I knew that she really didn't want to go anyway. She did tell me about Mrs. Salas accusing her of taking food from the house to feed Grover and Joseph—despite the fact she always prepared meals for them at home, even when they would be staying for a day or so. She wasn't sure how much of that she could take and began thinking more about getting her own restaurant and quitting that job. Between the money she had saved from working and the money we had in the apartment, she felt that she could probably make a go of it. It was fo' sho that she was the best cook I had ever seen, so it might just work out, sep fo' me not wanting to get rid of the farm.

Arriving back home this time was so different. I had never been here without the smell of tobacco from Papa's pipe or his big voice calling out to one of us. Anna seemed to be taking control of everything. She had made all the plans for Papa to be laid to rest. She even got the local preacher to come by the house to say some words while Papa's body was there.

Johnnie seemed to be taking Papa's death pretty hard too; I had never seen him so gloomy and down. He was typically the one with all the stories that made us all laugh, but now he just sat around not having much to say at all.

Concha came by from the other house, and of course she brought a dish or two even though there was plenty of food in the house. People from all over was stopping by just to pay their respects, and they all brought food with them. I was asked to get wine and liquor from the shed out back and bring it to the kitchen where we gathered.

We all sat around in the living room where Papa's casket was and told stories that were personal to each of us. I talked about the times we had in the fields, how no matter how hard I tried, I couldn't finish plowing and planting before him. I worked as hard as I could and Papa seemed to just be moseying along, but by the end of the day, he was done and waiting fo' me. He'd call out to me and ask if I needed help or something. I never could figure out how he did it. It was the mule, Johnnie said, and the whole room laughed. I had to laugh too. Papa did talk to that mule like he was a person; he even had a name fo' the animal.

We were having a good time talking about Papa, and it was good to see Johnnie and the others laughing. Some of the stories I had never heard before, and I found out foremost that Papa took to having a relationship with each one of us that was special to each one. There was no one mo' special than the other, even though you would think that you was the most important during the time he was with you.

We spent the entire day, late into the night, telling our stories and eating and drinking in between. We knew that tomorrow there would be a house full of people coming by to say their last goodbyes to Papa and our time alone as a family again would come to an end.

I could hardly sleep. I couldn't seem to want to believe that there would be no more times when I could sit with Papa and ask his advice on a matter or two or watch him interact with children, which he did so well. I thought, I will miss him, but the things he gave me, the instructions on living life, on being proud but not boastful, the lessons on how to conduct myself and on fairness toward all, on how to be a good man and to respect the woman in my life and women in general, those are the memories I'll have forever.

I awoke early to the smell of bacon and coffee; Concha was at it already, and I was feeling the hunger coming on. Later today there would be the service fo' Papa and they'd be taking him to the church and to the burial place. Although I was coming to peace with all of this, I still wasn't looking forward to this day. This makes it final; this is the end, sep fo' what I remember, I thought.

I went out to the back where there was already buckets of warm water waiting fo' whoever might need to wash up. I used the warm water to wash my face and hands so's I could get to the kitchen and to the food Concha had cooked fo' breakfast.

When I got to the kitchen, I was surprised to see that Johnnie was already there. "Good morning, sleepyhead," he said to me as I entered the kitchen. "You lucky I left you something to eat."

"I couldn't sleep, so I was up a lot later than you was," I said. "And I know Aunt Concha would never let even you eat all the food, no matter how greedy you are."

"Oh, sit down and eat while I still feel like letting you," Johnnie said. We both laughed.

We arrived at the big house midmorning, and the people had already started to come by 'fo' the service began. It was good to see some of the people I had not seen in some time. The smell of the different foods coming from the kitchen was a reminder of those days when Papa would have a cookout and people would bring the side dishes while he supplied the hog or the goat. There would be fried chicken and candy yams and cornbread and melons and all sort of food and drink. I knew, too, that Aunt Concha had made some peach cobbler, which was just the best ever. The preacher came in with his wife, and she had a large pan of food in her hand as she made her way to the kitchen where most of the woman were gathered.

He came over and asked me how I was doing as he shook me hand.

"Doing fine, sir," I answered, not wanting him to know that this was in fact the worst day of my life. He walked other to each of Papa's children, asking them the same question.

The service in the house was small. Even though there was standing room only, everybody got to pass by the casket and say goodbye. The men gathered 'round the casket and took it to the waiting carriage fo' the ride to the church.

The church was even mo' crowded. I had never seen this many people gathered together in one place befo'. There were even a few white folks there that I did remember from when me and Papa would take melons and corn and beans to town fo' the white folks to buy. We carried the casket to the front of the church and placed it on a table that was covered for the occasion. The preacher said some words as we placed the casket down on the table, and we turned to go to our seats in the front row of the church.

As I turned, I saw Josephine. I had not seen her in a very long time. I looked to her left and to her right. I knew that I would see Charles, Lula, and Frank, and there they were. My feelings went from anger to excitement quickly. It had not been a bad breakup. We still cared fo' each other, and even though I didn't understand why she just up and left, somehow, I felt it was not just of her doing. Nevertheless, I hadn't expected to ever see her or my children again, so the excitement was based on the fact that it happened this day: Papa was still giving even after death.

I tried to pay attention to the sermon. I could from time to time hear an "Amen" or a "Thank you, Jesus," but my mind was just not there. I was back there at a time when life was simple, when I worked the farm, tended to the livestock, and rested when it was all done. Papa and me would sit back and talk about the day's work and what was left to be done. Then I met Josephine, and it all changed.

1909

The farmhands were unloading off the wagon; they were the usual bunch that came from year to year to help pick the corn or melons that we would take to town and sell to the stores there. I knew most of them and could call them by name. Then I saw this pretty young girl I had never seen befo'. She was almost as tall has I was at the time, and she had the prettiest long legs. I could tell because she pulled up her dress so as not to trip getting off the wagon. I was stopped in my tracks—all I wanted to do was find out who she was.

Papa had to call out to me several times since I spent a good bit of my work time trying to see where she was instead of doing what I needed to do in the field. I was pretty much useless that whole day, but when it was time fo' the farmhands to leave, I was the first to reach their wagon. When she arrived, I quickly reached out my hand to her to help her up onto the wagon. I held her hand fo' a longer-than-needed time as I asked her her name.

"I'm Josephine," she said as I continued to hold her hand, "and I would very much like my hand back."

"Oh sorry, I just, well…I, um…"

"What is your name?" she asked as the wagon began to pull away.

I ran behind it and shouted, "Cleveland! My name is Cleveland."

I thought about her all the rest of that day and into the night. I wondered if she would be coming back tomorrow. I mean, what if I never see her again? I thought. I didn't get to find out if she was from here or if she was just visiting. After all, I have never seen her befo'; she may have been visiting some kinfolk and this was her last day so she spent it with them in the fields and I'll never get to see her again, I thought.

Each time I'd fall asleep, I just kept seeing her on that wagon going father and farther away from me as I ran as hard as I could to keep up to it but couldn't.

The dream went on until morning. I was glad to see the sun coming through the shutters. It meant that I did not have to continue with that same dream. I rushed out to the yard to claim a pail of water so that I could wash the sleep out of my eyes. I got dressed and went into the kitchen. I wanted to eat early and get out to the fields before the wagons began to come in fo' the day's work. I wanted to see Josephine again.

I could see the dust trail coming down the road. There were two wagons; they looked the same, so I didn't know if I should be closer to the first one or to the second one. I decided to stand in a position where I could see them both as they passed me by. That way I could see if she was on the first or the second and I'd be able to go to that one to help her off. I stood at my vantage point and watched fo' her, but I didn't see her at all from where I was standing. I knew it, I said to myself. She is no farm girl; she just did it yesterday to try it out, and I'm never gonna ever see her again.

I turned to head back to the field and had begun to walk away when I heard her voice calling my name. "Cleveland, you're not going to speak to me today?" she said softly.

I could feel my heart pounding faster than a jackrabbit in a trap. "No. I didn't see you getting off of the wagon, and I came here just so that I could see you get off the wagon," I said. "I was gonna go work myself to death since you weren't here."

"Do you say that to all the girls?" she said.

"No. I only wanted to see you get off of the wagon. Heck, the rest of these folks could have stayed home far as I'm concerned," I answered.

"Well, I better catch up with the others and get some work done," she said.

"Yeah, me too, 'fo' I get in trouble wit' Papa. He did say that I was spending mo' time looking yo' way yesterday than doing my share of the work. I can't do that again," I said.

"I'll see you later," she said as she turned and walked away.

"Fo' sho you will," I said as I headed fo' the melon field. She didn't see the big smile on my face, nor did she know how happy I was to see her again.

Josephine and I talked every day, and soon I got up the nerve to go to meet her folks. I was sho that this was the love of my life. Her folks seemed older that I had expected—came to find out that she was staying with her grandparents. There was some reason why that was, but she never talked about it, and whenever I would bring it up, she would shut down and not talk at all.

Mr. Warner was a bit of a tough old guy who did not mix words; he was straight to the point about things. One day I was sitting on the porch waiting fo' Josephine, and he outright asked me if I was having relations with Josephine. I was quick to answer that I was not, but the look he gave me told me that he didn't believe me fo' one second. I did realize that I was getting to the point where it was getting hard fo' me not to want to go further with her, and that's when I asked her to marry me. She said yes, and I quickly told Papa and Mr. Warner of my intentions. They were both good with it, and me and Josephine married.

Ten months later Charles was born, and a year after that, Lula was born, and the year after that, Frank was born, and it was shortly after that when she up and left without giving me a reason fo' why she wanted to do that to us. I knew that I worked hard and that sometimes it got to her having to tend to three babies and all, but I did all I could to make her happy. I didn't deserve her just leaving like that and tried to forget that it ever happened, so when I got the papers that we were no longer married, I tried to push her memory out of my mind. I did miss my children, though, and tried to find out where they were. No one seemed to know, or no one wanted to tell me.

"Cleveland, how many times do I have to call you?" I heard a voice saying. I looked up from my seat, and it was Anna. "Do you want to say something about Papa?" she asked. "Everyone else that wanted to have already talked."

"No. I just know that I'ma miss him so much, but I got the best of memories of all the things we did together, and that's just between him and me. Y'all's got yours, and I gots mine. No, I don't need to talk about that stuff."

I looked over to see if Josephine and the children were still there, and they were. I realized that I had pretty much missed the whole service thinking back on us and what happened to us. I wondered if I really wanted to know why she left know. I mean, I went on with my life, and she seems to be doing right well fo' herself. Why hash that stuff back up now? I thought.

"The Lord giveth, and the Lord taketh away. Blessed be the name of the Lord," the preacher said. "Philip led a good life, and now it's time for him to get his reward in heaven. Let the church say amen," he continued as the choir began to sing the song "He's Going Up Yonder." Papa always loved that song, and the woman singing the lead sang it so sweetly: "I'm going up yonder to be with my Lord." That was fittin' fo' Papa's send-off song. He sho believed in God and all, and he passed that on to us.

They buried Papa in a grave right behind the church. The preacher said a few mo' words from the good book, and they lowered him into the ground. It was that moment that I felt the less fo' knowing that he was fo' sho never gotta be there fo' me ever again sep in the things he taught me and the things we did together. I thought about that all the way back to the farm: Yep, this fo' real, just like when they finally told me that Mama was gone and wasn't coming back because she had died. There's just no coming back from that no matter how much crying you may have to do or the missing them you do.

When we got back to the big house, there was wall-to-wall people there, everyone from the church and mo'. There were people there that I hadn't seen since I was a little boy. I wanted to spend a little time with Josephine and the kids, but it was so hard to get around in the crowd of people. Each time I would find them in the crowd and try to make my way to them, someone would stop me and want to talk. I was about to just give up, but when I turned around, she had made her way to me. I took her by the hand and walked out the door to the backyard: that was the place with the fewest people.

"How you been?" I asked, almost afraid of what her answer might be.

"I been fine," she answered, showing the deep dimples on each cheek.

I gestured fo' her and the kids to sit on the bench Papa made fo' that area of the yard. He and I used to sit back there and talk on some days after working the fields. The kids were so much bigger than they were the last time I saw them; back then, Frank was just a little bitty thing. As I looked at them, I could feel the pain again coming up on me.

"I know you want to know what happened," Josephine said, as if she could see what was happening to me at that moment.

"I sho do," I said. "Fo' the life of me, I can't seem to find a good reason why you would just up and leave me like that. I just don't understand what could have made you do a thing like that. I wasn't bad to you; I didn't treat you in a bad way. I worked my fingers to the bone fo' you and these children, and you took them and left without a word or reason."

"I know I hurt you," she said as she took my hand and lead me toward the other end of the yard. "Children, y'all stay here while me and yo' daddy talk," she continued as we walked away from where the three children were seated.

My first thought was to just let her have a piece of my mind, just allow all the backed-up anger to come on out, but I somehow felt the need to just listen.

"I wanted to come home and tell you what was doing on," she began. "I went over to see bout Grandpapa as I would always do twice a week. He was sitting on the porch crying when we got there. I asked what had happened and he told me that my mama was very sick. He said that she was in such a bad way that he felt she wasn't going to make it but a week or so. He said that he had to get to her before she passed away and he wasn't sho just how he was going to do that, then he asked me to take him. He said that with me he wouldn't feel bad 'bout going that far. I wanted to say no and that I just couldn't leave home just like that, but he had the tickets already and the train was leaving round noon. I still didn't want to go, but he cried, and he told me that I could come back in a day or so. I didn't know that what I would find back home with my mama was a whole heap of trouble and that I'd be stuck smack-dab in the middle of it all.

"I came home and packed a bag fo' me and the churen while a wagon waited to take us to the train depot. After I got back home and saw the condition my mother was in, I knew that she needed me to stay and take care of her.

"The days turned to weeks and than to years. She finally passed away, but by then I knew that you had to move on, so I got the divorce so you could be free to find someone fo' yo'self. I'm so sorry fo' the pain I caused you and specially fo' keeping yo' churen from you. I just knew that you could never fo'give me fo' that, but when I heard that yo' daddy had died, I hoped that you would allow me to come by and pay my respects to him. He was such a nice man, and he treated me real well fo' all the time I knowed him. I hope you ain't angry with me fo' coming; I don't want to cause you any mo' pain than I already did.

"I talked to them every day and told them about their daddy. Charles and Lula got yo' looks, and Frank, he kinda looks mo' like me, sep for that nose. All yo' churen got yo' nose, that big o' wide thing," she said with a small smile.

I still wasn't sho how I felt bout things even after hearing the whole story. I reckon it's better than her leaving me fo' another man o' some such thing, and no matter what I can't do much bout the past that's so far gone, I said to myself. I was getting ready to speak when I heard Johnnie called to me from the back door.

"Cleveland, come here fo' a minute," he said in a voice that made it sound as if there was a bit of a problem.

"I'll be right there," I shouted back toward the door. That's when Johnnie saw me and Josephine.

"I won't keep you too long," he said, looking at me and her. "It should only take a minute to tell these women what we plan to do."

I looked at Josephine and told her that we would talk again later. I wasn't sho what Johnnie was talking about, but I figured that I had better get in there before he got me tangled up in something I didn't want to be tangled in.

"OK," Josephine said. "I do think you had better get in there. We'll talk again soon."

I made my way over to where Johnnie was standing. When I got there, he quickly put his arm around my shoulder. I knew from the past that when he did that, there was something up. Now I began to wonder what he had gotten me into this time.

As I looked 'round the kitchen, I saw Ms. Clara sitting in her usual chair at the table and Anna sitting to her right. Johnnie walked me Papa's seat and pulled it out fo' me to sit. This was getting to feel mo' and mo' like something I didn't want no part of.

Johnnie sat at the other end of the table and began to talk as soon as he sat down. "Look, everybody," he began, "now, we know that this farm is gonna be too much fo' Ms. Clara, and the girls can't do the upkeep, much less manage the farming, so as I see it, Cleveland, if you and Hattie and yo' two boys move back here—and of course you surely know all there is about farming—everything will be good. Now, Anna thinks that it would be a good thing to sell off some of this and keep the house and the land around it."

"Wait a minute," I said. "I can't say that I can get my wife to ever want to live on a farm. She just ain't a farm girl; she really hates this place, so I can't say that yo' plan is a good one at all."

"See, I told you," Anna said. "I said that we need to look at selling off some of the land and keep what Mama Clara wants around the house."

"How much of the farmland is in use right now, and what about any crops that we need to get to market?" I asked. "I can't see us thinking 'bout selling anything until I take a good look at what Papa has done and what still needs to be done."

"Ha ha, I told you," Johnnie said. "Cleveland will take care of the farm, and we don't have to sell off anything."

"Hold up," I said. "I didn't say that I was gonna take over the farm; that's not what I said at all. I just want to look 'round and get and idea as to what needs to be done 'round here. That's all I can promise to do at this time. I reckon it should take me a day or so, then I need to get back home to my wife and kids."

"There, it's all settled," Johnnie said. "Cleveland will figure it all out, and we go from there."

I wasn't so sure that I liked the sound of that. He is almost saying he is putting this whole thing on me, I thought. I looked at Ms. Clara, wanting to hear from her, and she smiled.

We settled on me taking a day to look 'round the farm to get an idea of what Papa had been doing. I would check the fields and the barns fo' any signs of things that needed to be attended to. We talked fo' a while, and I could tell that Ms. Clara was glad to know that I would check things out; that made me happy. She was always very nice to me, and I felt this might be a way to pay her back fo' that.

When we was done, I realized that there was only a few people left at the house. Most of them were from the small farms up the road. They stepped into the kitchen to say their farewells to us and to wish us a safe journey back to our homes. I also realized that Josephine and the kids was gone and I hadn't gotten to talk to them. Maybe I'll see them before I leave fo' home in a day or two, I thought.

It had been a long day, and I had to admit that I was looking forward to walking round the farm tomorrow; it had been a while since I had to do that. I lay there wondering just what I was gonna find that needed to be done and wondering just how long it would take fo' me to get it done.

As I walked out the door, the wind was blowing harder than I had ever heard it blow befo'. This was the hand of God moving throughout the land. I looked 'round, trying to find where the house used to be; there was nothing there. The trees were coming outta the ground, and all the earth was turning and blowing in the wind. A big black cloud was coming 'cross the sky. I began to run, but I wasn't getting anywhere. It was as though I were not running at all, sep that I knew I was running, trying to outrun that black cloud as it came over my body. The next thing I knew, I was looking down on the land from way up in the sky. The house was there, and the land was filled with all kinds of crops, and the trees were filled with fruit. Then I began to fall back to earth. I screamed.

I sat up in the bed. It was all a dream, and as I looked toward the window, I could see that the sun was about to come up. What a dream, I thought. What does it mean? Papa used to say that there was meaning in the things we dream, and that dream was too real to not mean something.

I could smell the bacon and the crackling bread that was cooking on the stove. Hattie was a great cook, but she never made crackling bread. I knew that the one place to get such a meal fo' breakfast like this was here on the farm. I was getting pretty hungry just thinking about the warm bread coming outta the pan and me taking that first bite. I rushed out to the yard and made my way to the outhouse 'cross the little stream. I wanted to hurry back and wash up and get to the breakfast table.

"Morning, Aunt Concha," I said as I sat at the large table. I was surprised that I was the only one up and that Johnnie didn't beat me to the table

"Morning, Cleveland," Aunt Concha said. "Yo' brother done ate and made his way over to the big house. He said that you could meet him there whenever you got up."

I should have known I never could beat him at most anything, even getting up and out to work. I reckon some things just never change. I ate my breakfast, went back to my room, and made the bed before walking over to the big house. I thought, On the way I'll look over the fields 'tween here and there and see if much planting's been done. After stopping by the house, I'll walk the rest of the land and see what's been done over there. That will give me an idea of what I'll be up against and how I'll need to go 'bout it, thought my biggest problem won't be getting the farm straightened out; it will be how to tell Hattie and what she'll say 'bout it. I'm not so sure 'bout how that's gonna turn out—probably not so good fo' me—but I sho do miss her and the kids, that's fo' sho.

On the train ride home, I couldn't take my eyes offin the porters I saw at the stations. There was something 'bout them that I really liked; I wondered if I'd be able to do what they did if I had the chance. And those uniforms that made them look so sharp and dandy—I think that I'd wear that well, I thought. Ah well, that's just a thought that will never come to pass. I have a wife and kids to look out fo', and some of those porters have to stay away from home fo' long periods of time, and my Hattie ain't puttin up with that fo' a minute of time, much less days.

I reached home befo' sundown. Since it was a weekday, I thought that there would be someone home even if Hattie had to work, but the house was empty. I could tell that she knew that I was coming home when I looked in the icebox and there was plated food there. It was the same as when she knew that I was coming home, and she'd be out. All I'd have to do is heat it up. I noticed that there was mo' than one plate there, so maybe she thought that I'd should have been home sooner.

I heated up the food and sat down at the kitchen table to eat. In a way I was a bit glad that she wasn't there: it gave me some time to figure out just how to explain to her that I was going to quit my job and go back to that farm until we figured out what to do with it. I knew that my chances were slim to none that she'd be just fine with that. Fo' sho that would not be the case, but there was no one even half as good as me when it came to tending the land. And I knew that at some point we were going to sell bits and pieces of it off and split the money 'tween us, but until that day came, I could work the land like Papa did and sell the harvest just as he did. Heck, I done went with him so many times that I knows just what to do and what to say, I thought. I can send money here to Hattie and the boys, and I can come down fo' times to be with them. That could work.

This was how I was thinking in my own head; it fo' sho might not have been any way that Hattie would think of it. It would leave her with taking care of the boys on her own, and there lay the problem. I sho wish there was another way outta this mess. I needs a way that don't burden her. Good Lord, help me, I thought.

I cleaned up the kitchen and went into the living room. By now the quiet was beginning to get to me. I wished that Hattie and the boys would come on home so's I could see them. I realized that I missed them all and didn't really like not being with them, yet I was going to have to be away from them fo' weeks at a time. I lay across the couch, just wanting to end the way I was feeling, and I fell asleep.

The knock on the door was the loudest I had ever heard; it was as if whosoever was knocking was using a heavy stick. On the farm I would have gone fo' my gun, but I didn't keep a gun in this house. I walked slowly toward the door, wondering if I was making the right decision to just answer it. From the sound of the knocking, I had a bad feeling about what was on the other side.

As I arrived at the door, I heard the word "Police" after another knock. I could not fo' the life of me figures out why a policeman would be knocking on my door. Now my urge was to find out what this was all about. I opened the door, and there stood a tall white man with a pink-cheek face standing with a bat-like stick in his hand. "Are you Cleveland Golden?" he asked.

"That be me," I answered. "What seems to be the matter?"

"Do you have a wife named Hattie and a couple of boys?" he asked.

"I sho do," I said, "And why is you asking, Mister, 'bout them? Is they all right?"

"They're, in a hospital, and the woman—Hattie—well, she been calling your name over and over, again and again."

"Cleveland, Cleveland. Are you all right, Cleveland? Wake up." I opened my eyes to see Hattie standing over me. "Are you OK?" she asked. "I been calling you, and you looked like you were having a really bad dream."

I looked over at the door and saw Grover and Joseph. "I'm fine now," I said as I got up and gave her a big hug and kiss. I called the boys over and hugged them too. "I missed you all," I said, "and it's so good to be home."

That night we spent just talking about what had been going on, me about Papa's funeral and Hattie about what had been going on with the boys and her job.

I didn't want to spoil the night by talking about going back to the farm before I got it squared away. We were enjoying our time together, and though I knew I would have to talk about it at some time soon, fo' sho this was not going to be the time.

We put the children to bed and got ready fo' bed ourselves. I knew that I would have to give notice to my boss tomorrow and figured that this was as good a time as any to tell Hattie also. I watched her as she got ready for bed. She always tied a sash around her head, which was the very last thing before getting into bed.

I waited for her to come to bed and softly said to her, "I need to talk to you about the farm."

She leaned over and kissed me. "I know you have to go back for a while, but not tonight you don't," she said as she reached fo' me.

CHAPTER 5

1924

Most of the land had been sold off; there was little more than four acres left. The hard times getting to this point had cost me my marriage. I tried coming home as much as I could, but the farm was a bigger thing to handle than Hattie could stand. I still got down there to spend time with the boys and continued with their support.

This was also a time to get to know my other children. They were at the farm almost every weekend, and I did get to bond with them. Charles and Frank would come over and help out with the summer and fall harvest. Frank reminded me of myself when I was younger: he seemed to like getting involved in all aspects of farming. Charles was good at doing whatever he was asked to do.

They were both great help. Lola helped out when she was needed but mostly spent time around the big house tending to the garden. She really liked growing things; it was nothing for her to plant a whole mess of blackberries or 'matoes or even strawberries. She'd be so excited to bring them into the house to show them off. We'd all clap fo' her when she brought in a big strawberry or a big ripe tomato to show her handiwork.

Although it was a good time getting to know them, I knew that sooner or later, I was going to have to figure out just what I was going to do with my life. Ms. Clara, Sista Emma, and Sista Sarah were all settled on the four acres of land they wanted to hold on to. Aunt Concha was settled in the other house on the two acres there, and she had even taken in a boarder who helped tend the land as well as fix things around the house. Everyone seemed to be doing quite well sep me. I needed to get a move on and find a place to dig in and make my mark. Workin' the trains might be a start, I thought.

1925

I looked into the mirror fo' the fourth time; I was sho looking good in my dark-blue uniform. I blew a breath on the shiny badge on my cap and wiped it with my handkerchief. I wanted to improve the shine if I could so's everybody would see it from a distance. I made my way down to the station in the pickup truck I bought to use on the farm. The plan was to keep a room at the small house fo' the times I'd be in the area and when I was in another town, find out where the other porters stayed at those times. I figured I'd be able to save money while also being able to look in on the family to make sho they's all right.

We colored porters had a small room in the back of the station where we could sit iffin we were waiting fo' the next train to come in. There was an old porter named Herbert. I kinda liked him a lot; he'd always give me pointers on how to act and what to do as a part of the job. Some of it I thought was silly, but I never told him that. He'd say always smile and say yes sir and yes ma'am. I didn't mind the yes sir and the yes ma'am. What I didn't like was the smiling part. Iffin my feet be hurting like he said his was, I wasn't so sho that I'd wanna be smiling.

My fist week went well, or so's I thought. I cleared a whole dollar and fifteen cents in tips. I coulda made even mo' iffin I ran to the next passenger as I saw two other porters doing—in fact one, Herbert, almost knocked me over getting past me to pick up the bags of two white folks. I told him that I was gonna knock-kick his ass iffin he did that again. Herbert told me that I would only lose my job iffin I did that; he told me to instead just be a little bit faster at getting the people through the station and that would increase my speed so's I could get to the next passenger quicker. It took me a couple of days to get it down, but befo' long, I was the quickest bag handler in the station, and it paid off.

After four months I was asked if I wanted to work the rails. That would mean I'd be going on the trains and doing the entire run. I'd be assigned to the Norfolk Southern Railway and go to the many stops that it made. Herbert told me that that was where the real money was. He said that I could clear mo' than five or six dollars a trip and I'd get time off with the rest of the train crew.

Making mo' money was what I heard: I wanted to someday be able to buy me a good piece of land and get back to what I did best. So, I accepted the job with a look to my future.

Over the next few weeks, I as in towns I'd never heard of and some I'd only heard white folks talking 'bout. There was Charlotte, North Carolina, where I stayed in a small colored hotel that had a band on the weekends playing in its dining hall. There was Norfolk, Virginia—I damn near got myself lynched down there fo' eyeballing a white couple just 'cuz she was so tall and he was trying to keep up with her stride. I thought they looked funny; he thought I shouldn't have been looking at his woman the way I was. He caused a ruckus, and as the crowd grew, I was made to take my leave by one of the other porters.

I found that I really liked to travel the rail. I wasn't so sure about all the places I would have to lay over in, though, and I was very sho that I didn't like the big city with all the crowding and stuff. I knew a little about such places, having lived in Savannah, but some of the cities were much worse, with the wall-to-wall people and the motorcars. I was always the happiest when I knew I'd be heading back to South Carolina and the calm that was home. There were times when I wondered just how much more of it I could take, then I realized that I had been saving money and would be able to buy a nice piece of land and settle down; that would bring the joy back to my life and give me what I needed to continue on this way.

I also missed the children, who were all in school and growing as tall as trees. It was always a joy when I could get to Savannah and see the boys. The train line didn't go there, so I would have to drive down or take the train from South Carolina to go to see them.

After six years on the rail, I had a savings of mo' than 310 dollars. I had also met a wonderful woman named Martha. She was the prettiest woman I had seen in a while. I saw her waiting fo' the rain to stop coming outta the colored store. At first, I wondered what she was doing on this side of town; I was sho that she was a white woman with her silky, shiny black hair, which fell down onto her clear light skin. I didn't want any trouble, so I was sho not gonna say anything to her.

She had two bags filled to the rim with groceries, and she asked me to help her. I could then tell by her voice that she was not a white woman. She had a deep Southern drawl and spoke every bit like black women I had known all my life. I took the bags from her so that she could get to her purse. After pulling out a coin fo' the bus, she stretched out her arms to receive the bags back.

"How about I give you a lift home with these bags and you won't need to worry about getting on the bus?" I spoke.

Martha looked me over. I could see that she was trying to see what kind of person I was and if she'd be all right in my company. "I assure you my intentions are good," I said. "I only want to be a help to you, and you don't really want to get that hair of yours all wet, now do you?"

"OK," she said, holding back the smile from my mentioning her hair. "Just a lift home and nothing else."

"That's all I'm here to do," I said while walking toward the bench the outside the store. "You wait here, and I'll drive around and pick you up. My car is just around the corner, so it should not take but a minute," I added I showed her to the seat.

She sat down, and I put the bags next to her. "Be right back," I said as I rushed away, wanting to get back as soon as I could. I wanted to know more about her.

I drove her to the house she was staying at. It was about three miles up the road. She didn't talk much, so I had to do most of the talking. Just small stuff—I didn't want to scare her away the very first time I was alone with her.

I helped her outta my truck and took the packages to the front door and waited to see if she'd invite me in. She opened the door, took the bags from my hand, and thanked me fo' the ride, then closed the door. I felt that I'd struck out, but as I made my way to the truck, she called out to me.

"If you want, you can see me again," she said.

"I sho 'nough would like that," I called back to her.

"Tomorrow, at six," she said. "I'll be here ready."

"That's right fine with me," I said as I turned away so's she couldn't see the big grin on my face. I looked out the back window, and she was still there. I waved goodbye.

I couldn't wait to see her again, and when I went to pick her up that next day, I had on my finest clothes and was carrying a box of chocolates. I took her out to eat, and we talked and talked. After the night was over, I felt like I had known her my whole life. I told her my dream of one day buying some land and getting back to farming; she seemed to like the idea as much as I did. We decided that it would be a goal of ours and started to plan how to go about it. Martha was book smart and worked in an office building. I had to get back on the rail. We figured it would take a year before we could start looking fo' land to buy. I'd build a house on it, and we would get married.

It took two years and seven months befo' we saw the land in Pineland, South Carolina.

1929

I could tell that Martha was getting tired of waiting fo' me to get off the railroad; we had not planned on it taking so long. The land in Pineland was twelve and a half acres and was owned by Martha's family. They were willing to let us buy the land and pay it off as we went, but I wanted to buy it outright. I looked it over every time I came home and had a few days. I knew just where I'd build the house and what I would do with the rest of the land. The problem was the trees—there was so many trees.

I drove into the nearby towns and searched fo' the woodwork companies. There were a few: Harold's Wood Company in Ridgeland, and Smith and Sons in Elkton. I'd get in touch wit' both so's they'd have to compete wit' each other fo' the wood. I reckoned I could pull together a crew of my own to help wit' the build of the house and get the wood companies to cut the wood I'd need as part of the deal.

The house was done by mid-September. It had taken over a year to complete. I was taking my last railroad trip; I knew Martha was at the breaking point and if I didn't get this marriage done soon, I was gonna lose the woman. I stopped in a jewelry store in Maryland and bought a fine diamond ring and wedding band. As soon as I get home, I'm gonna seal this down with Martha and make it official; we's getting married, I thought.

I had already told the company that I was leaving. The other porters threw a little party fo' me at one of the hotels we stayed at when we were on the road. I was sho to keep the rings in my pocket since I knowed that there were people who would go into the rooms when nobody was there and steal from the porters. I was sho not to drink the white lightnin' they served 'cause story was that they'd put something in yo' drink and you wouldn't have no memory of what happened to you or yo' money. I didn't want to seem outta place, so I stayed at the party watching all the goings-on but not doing mo'.

I made it through the night and the party. It was nice to think that someone thought enough of you to want to show it that way, even though I do believe that most of the purple there was there just to drink and have fun. It probably didn't matter much who the party was fo'. I did hear some screaming coming from the hotel when I was leaving. Someone was saying that their money was missing. It sounded like one of the men I saw drinking and talking to one of the women who hung around the hotel. He was treating to kill everybody in the place if he didn't get his money back. I was glad that I had played it as I did—I still had my money and the rings.

It would be over three hours be fo I got offin this train and into a new life where I could get back to working the land. I was looking forward to it and to marrying Martha. It seemed like the longest time in the world. I looked at myself in the mirror. Boy, did I look sharp in my uniform, hat rim shiny and buttons gleaming. After today this will be over and done—no mo' lifting and carrying people's bags, no mo' waking people up with trays of food so's they can eat in their cabins, no mo' wondering if they's gonna give you a penny or a dime. I'll be my own man wit' my own land, answering to no one septin my wife, I thought as I began my rounds.

The train pulled into Yemassee. I had all the bags near the exit as the passengers began to leave the train. I would watch fo' which one they'd point at and pick it up as they left the train. I would put it down where the outside porters could take it. My tip would usually come when I moved the bags from the cabin, so as I put one bags down, I moved on to the next, doing that until all of the passengers had left the train. This time the only difference would be that after I got all of them off, I would be leaving too, so the last bag was mine. I took it into the room in the back and changed.

1930

In had been a month in the planning—Martha and me was getting married. The house was completed as we had wanted. We'd be married at the local church and have a reception at the house, where Concha and a few other women were cooking and setting up all the fixings.

I was dressed in my finest suit of clothes and waiting at the altar, Johnnie and Willy by my side, when the music played, and I could see Martha coming down the aisle. The closer she got, the more beautiful she got. I wondered fo' a moment if I was really this lucky to have such a pretty woman fo' my wife. Soon she was by my side, and we said our I dos. It was real.

We drove back to the house, and I picked her up and carried her over the threshold, kissing her as we crossed into our new lives. It seemed everyone was waiting fo' us to arrive befo' most of the eating began. I went into the kitchen area and asked what the problem was and why nobody was eating. The women looked at me as if I had said something crazy.

"Ain't nobody s'pose to do no eating until you and yo' bride gets here," Aunt Concha said. "Now let's get her in here, and we can start serving."

I looked around fo' Martha, only to find her still in the living room talking to some of the friends and family members who were sitting around. I was glad that they at least had drinks in their hands; I would have hated to think that they had to wait fo' that too.

I finally got her attention and had her to go into the kitchen so's we could get some food in these people. Drinking without eating could cause a heap of trouble the very next day, and I didn't want to be the cause of that. Also, I myself was 'bout ready to pass out from not eating, so's I wanted it to hurry up. 'Fo' long everybody was eating.

The gathering went way long into the evening. I fo' one wished it hadda ended a good bit earlier, but Martha was having such a good time that I really didn't mind so much. There was a good bit of food left, so we tried to get everyone to take a plate or two home with them, and most did.

The last to leave was three ladies from the church up the road a piece. Martha and me had been attending that church fo' a while, since we knowed we'd be needing a place to go to church when we settled into our new home. They stayed and helped to clean up the kitchen and stow away the food that was left.

It would be four days befo' we'd see anyone else at the house. That day, one of the neighbors from the farm off to the right of the wooded area came by to introduce himself. I wondered why I hadn't seen him while I was building the house, but I thought not to ask—I was sho there must have been a reason. I called to him to come on up to the porch and grab a seat. On the way up, I noticed that he had a real bad limp. It was really hard fo' him to make his way up the three stairs that led up to the porch. I figured out why he hadn't come over.

When the man finally got to the seat, he was nearly out of breath.

"Could I get you a glass of water?" I asked the rather frail man.

"Nope. I's pretty good, just want to let you know who yo' neighbor is. I's Samual Jenkins. Me and my wife Eli lives just beyond those trees over yonder," he said as he pointed toward the woods.

"I knowed you been workin on the house fo' some time, but I was not able to get much until two days ago, so I thought it was as good a time to come and say welcome to ya. I woulda come sooner, but I been ill a bit and couldn't get 'round much."

"I thank ya fo' coming. My name is Cleveland Golden, and my wife is named Martha. Is you sho you don't want a drink of water? I's gonna get me one since it's piping hot out today."

"Thank ya, Cleveland, I think I will have that drink.

We talked fo' bout three hours. It seemed that Mr. Jenkins knew a lot about the area and all the towns surrounding the farms. He was once a cotton and corn farmer; those was the crops he made the most money on. He knew all the cotton mills and the names of the owners and managers of each of them. He knew who was apt to try and cheat you and who would give a fair price fo' the crops.

These were things I needed to know since I wasn't sho which crops I should be looking to plant first spring. I had planned to plant my beans in the patch of land over to the right of the house, and there was still a bit of work to finish the backyard. I told Samuel that I'd take him back to his place and asked if he'd be able to sit with me some mo' sometime soon. He agreed to that, and I drove him the little ways to his house.

"Thank ya again fo' yo' coming by. If there be anything I can do fo' ya, just ask," I said after Samuel left the car.

"I'll be talking to you soon," he answered.

I went home and talked to Martha 'bout the talk I had had wit' Samuel. We both saw how he could be a good help to us as we wanted to know mo' 'bout the area and maybe even get mo' land. I felt that Samuel could show me 'round the nearby towns so's I could pick out who I wanted to deal wit' as the farm began to grow.

It was settled that I was gonna take the time needed to get as much information from the man as I could while also building relationships in the area. I called on Samuel two days later and asked if he'd mind showing me round. He quickly agreed: I think he also liked the idea that I had a motorcar and that he liked riding in it.

Samuel and me rode around from town to town fo' the next few weeks. He showed me where the markets that would buy farm products by the season were. He showed me where the mills were and talked about the owners and if they were fair-minded or not. We rode through the towns where workers could be found to do the seasonal pickins and who were the best at the job. Each night I would talk to Martha about what the day was like, all that I had seen and heard. She agreed to make the return trip with me to all the places since she was book learned and could make note of things that I would need to know as I did my daily trading.

Martha packed a lunch, and we when into town, first to Ridgeland, where I showed her the places I could sell to the common markets and such. She took out a pencil and paper and wrote down words as I told her what

Samuel had told me about the places. We drove another bit yonder to the next town; I showed her the places that me and Samuel looked at there, and she took out the paper again and wrote down words. On the way to the next town, we saw a place where we could stop and spread out a blanket and have some lunch. There was a bit of trees and a pond of water running through it. I carried the basket of food as Martha laid down the blanket. It was there that she told me that she was with child.

"Is you fo' sho?" I asked, not fo' a minute thinking befo' saying the words.

"I'd know a thing like that," she quickly answered, with a look that I had never seen befo'.

"I guess I should be asking is you all right fo' all this riding," I said.

"I'm fine," she answered with a much mo' pleasant look than the one I'd been given befo'.

"We can turn 'round and go home iffin you want," I said.

"I'm OK to go on," she said. "It'll we some time before I need to rest more, so it's best that we go now, and I can collect all of the information I'll need to help you with this in the future."

We finished lunch and continued to the next town. I showed her the mills, and she again wrote words on her paper. On the trip home, she told me that she had the names and addresses of each of the places we had gone to. She suggested that we talk to other farmers who might have done business with these people so that we could get an idea of whether they were fair-minded or not and how they treated colored folk.

I thought that the best place to start was back with Samuel: he knew a lot, and he knew a lot of people. Martha suggested that we have them over fo' dinner. That way she would be able to ask the questions that were on her mind. I told her that I'd go see him tomorrow and see when it would be good fo' him and his wife to come over.

For the next few days, I spent a lot of time with Samuel and Eli. We had them over fo' dinner and the next day fo' lunch. There was a lot of questions that Martha had that I'd never even thought 'bout. Would we have to pick people up in wagons to pick crops? Did we need to deliver items to the mills, or did they come and check out the products first and then send someone to pick them up? These were all questions that I never thought to ask, but Martha did, and we sho needed to know all this befo' we set out to do all this work not knowing what we needed to make it work out right.

Next Samuel took me to meet some of the other farmers. They didn't seem to mind talking to me since none were anywhere near where I was coming from and some only dealt in one or two items. They told me who would be the most likely to try and cheat colored folk and who would pay a good price. None knew what white folks got.

It was not long befo' I got the hang of it as I took my first corps to market. I had potatoes, yams, and peanuts. Two markets tried to undercut my price, which was a good price. I ended up making the best deal with Harris and Sons. As time went by, I would just ride right on past the other markets with a full load on my wagon, just a-hoping that they see me through the windows.

By the time the farm was in full swing, and I was planting corps fo' every season, I had good relations with the top buyers in the towns around the farm. James and Cleveland Jr. had been born, and Martha was four months pregnant.

Martha had been going to the markets with me in the beginning but now had to spend most of her time at home with the boys. Mr. Jenkins would take the ride with me iffin he was feeling well enough, which was not very often. I learned my way around and was able to, from time to time, hire local folks to help in the fields with picking cotton and pulling up yams and potatoes. That was a big help to some of the people in the area: I'd give them a good wage fo' a good day's work.

The farm was getting bigger. We owned another twenty-six acres by the time Herbert was born. I had to build a storage shack, a large bin fo' the hay and feed fo' the mule, and a bigger chicken hut with shelves to give them space fo' laying and hatching eggs. Yep, it was becoming the farm I always dreamed I'd have one day.

One season Mr. Jenkins got very sick and near died. Martha looked after his wife, who was sickly too, and I took him back and forth to the doctor fo' medicine and such. It took a long while, but Mr. Jenkins did start to get better. The bank was coming after his bit of land, though. They said that he still owed money and that they were going to make him leave so's they could sell the four acres off.

I talked with Martha about it; we were not going to let the bank just kick them off the land, so we looked to buy it. Martha got the legal things together, and we brought the place. We told the Jenkinses that they could stay there as long as they wanted to. It was a good feeling knowing that we did that.

Mr. Jenkins got much better and would often ride with me to the markets. He was really good at setting them white folks straight on prices and such. I was glad to have him as a friend. Martha reminded me of how they stuck with us after Philip III died and we were both so down in the dumps. He was only five years old and got so sick with fever and such. We weren't so sure that we ever wanted another child, but Martha was pregnant again and we is both happy that she was.

The farm was still growing. We were able to buy another eleven acres of land on the other side of the stream. It was ideal fo' planting in the summer since I was able to direct the water to the crops. I began growing corn and cotton over there. When the first crops came that year, it was the highest moneymaking year we ever had, and I was able to buy a pickup truck that allowed me to bring the fruits and vegetables from the fields to the house much mo' easy. The car could'n hold as much, and we liked to have enough on hand to give to the folks who came by with a need fo' it. Martha would make preserves with the fruits, and I'd make a barrel or two of wine fo' drinking round the holidays and such as folk wanted a sip now and then.

That patch of land was good fo' planting sugarcane. Heck, I was making so much syrup that when word got out, folks from all over would come by the farm to see iffin I'd sell some to them. I sold a little bit, but mostly I gave it away. I didn't want know trouble wit' the government or them people thinking I was selling whiskey or something.

I must admit there was a bit of a liquor still going on in the evening while I made syrup, but it was just enough fo' me to have a bit to taste on in the evening afo' going to bed—there ain't nothing like having a bit of corn liquor from time to time.

When Herbert was born, Johnnie, Mr. Jenkins, and Cornelia all were at the house. It was good to see both Johnnie and Cornelia at the same time. My brother would be able to make it out to the farm, but my sister would not be able to make it at those times. Cornelia took over the kitchen while Martha got a bit of rest. I do believe this was the hardest birthing she had ever been through. She screamed fo' many a hours befo' he came outta her, and boy, was he a big baby.

Martha came into the living room, where we were, at with the baby in her arms. I could see the wear in her face and wondered what I could do to help her. When I asked, she quickly handed me the large baby. There was something about holding him that made me feel good. I rocked him until he went to sleep. Martha came back from the kitchen and went to reach fo' him; I didn't want to let him go. Johnnie laughed at me, not wanting to let go even after Martha had him in her arms again. Johnnie poured me another drink.

CHAPTER 6

1939

The early harvest was almost over. There was plenty of potatoes, yams, and pecans fo' the market. The boys had done well helping out with the packing and picking, so they were to go along with me to the store to get some of the candy they liked. I dropped the haul off at the four places that had ordered it and stopped at the seed house to pick up a bag of cottonseed.

On the way to the seed house was the only store that would let us colored folk in to buy sweets. The boys knew just what it was that they wanted, so we were in and out of there in nearly no time at tall.

The boys were out of school fo' the summer, so this was the beginning of the time we'd have to spend together. It really wouldn't be much because I would soon be back to planting the summer crops: the watermelons and tomatoes on into the beans that needed planting by summer's end. There was a music show coming to town in a few days.

James shouted out as he read the words on the large poster with the picture on it, "Could we go to hear the music, Papa?"

Junior shouted out the same following his brother.

"When is it?" I asked, watching as he did count on his fingers.

"In ten days," he said, "right up near the white folks' church."

"OK. You just be sure to remind me befo' the day comes," I said.

"I sure will, Papa," James answered. "I sure will."

Junior shook his head in agreement as we made our way outta town, heading home.

I was sitting on the porch having a smoke when I saw the dust from a car coming down the road off the main roadway. From the dust it was kicking up, I could tell whoever it was wanted to reach here in a hurry.

It wasn't long 'fo' I could see that it was Johnnie's car. I hadn't seen him since Herbert was born, and I didn't 'spect ta see him now. I could only wonder what the reason was that he'd just show up like this. As he pulled up to the house and got out of the car, I could almost feel that there was something just not right: his head was down, and he seemed not to want to look me in the eye.

"What brings you all the way here?" I asked as he climbed the three stairs to the porch.

"I'm glad you sitting down, cuz I just got the worst news to tell ya," he said with a look on his face like I had never seen befo'.

"Could I get you a drink?" I asked.

"Yeah, a good stiff one at that," he said.

I got up and went inside to get a bottle of corn liquor I kept in the house. Johnnie followed me in. I called out to Martha; she was in the kitchen. The boys were playing 'round the side of the house. Since it was near suppertime, I told Martha that Johnnie was here and to be sho to fix a place fo' him at the dinner table.

I brought the bottle and two glasses to the living room, where Johnnie had seated himself. I handed him a glass and the bottle and watched as he poured himself a good drink.

"OK, what's going on?" I asked and waited fo' him to take another sip of the drink befo' he began to speak.

"He done killed her," Johnnie said. "That son of a bitch killed Cornelia, shot her dead."

"What are you talking 'bout?" I asked. "Cornelia ain't been married long. Who killed her?"

"That son-of-a-bitch husband of hers shot her full of bird shot. They say they was arguing, and he put his hand on her and she went toward the kitchen and he went fo' the shotgun. He followed her into the kitchen wit' the shotgun, and she pulled a kitchen knife, and he just shot a big old hole in her chest."

I didn't realize that I was crying until Martha wiped the tears from my face. Cornelia was just younger than me, and I always had to look out fo' her, 'specially when boys came a-courting. I remember one boy I sho' nough didn't like and I made sure that he never came back to try and see her again; I couldn't tell her what I did, but it was fo' her own good. I poured myself a drink and asked if her husband was in jail.

"No. He's on the run, and I don't trust that the police is trying real hard to find him iffin you ask me," he said.

"Where is she?" I asked, knowing that she lived a good three or so hours from here.

"She's at the Styila Funeral Home. They's waiting fo' what we want to do," Johnnie said. "I told them that I had to get wit' my family and I'd get back to them in a day or so."

"We's gonna take her home," I said, realizing that I was talking to my older brother, whom I always looked up to and gave the final say. Somehow, I felt that he wanted me to take the lead on this; he knew just how close me and Cornelia was.

I decided not to tell the boys until I figured out all the details. I knew it would probably cut into the music show, but something like that could be made up later. I was pretty sho that they would understand. They had grown to love their auntie Cornelia and the fine baking she would do whenever we got together.

At dinner there was not the usual chatter that was a part of Johnnie coming over to visit. The boys could almost tell that something was wrong as we ate in silence.

The service was quick and simple. Outside of the family, there was three woman who knew Cornelia and said that they were friends of hers and there was a man who was well-dressed but said very little about how he knew her. He did seem to be genuinely upset by her passing; even though he didn't say much, you could see it on his face. I think I even saw him cry a bit while the preacher was talking about her.

She was buried near Mama's and Papa's graves. Martha, knowing that we were going there, brought flowers for both graves even though she never knew anything about them except what I might have said or what might have been said by Johnnie or Cornelia when they came to visit us at the farm. She also held me tightly when the casket was being lowered into the ground. I just couldn't help but cry fo' my sister, whom I remembered playing the most with as a child. I knew that I was going to miss her a lot.

Three weeks had gone by since we buried Cornelia, and I had to get back to the daily business of running the farm. It was not an easy thing to do since I just couldn't get myself together. The boys were a big help as they took on more responsibility for doing the chores of packing fruit and veggies fo' the market. I was glad to have them step up fo' this, although I wasn't quite ready to let them go out on their own to make the sales. I didn't want them white folk to take advantage of them and have to go back and make it right, so I'd still made the trip even though I didn't want to be bothered with no white folks since they didn't seem to be finding that killer man.

It was sometime befo' I took back to feeling somewhat normal about being around white folk again. After all, they paid good money fo' my products and there would be no way to get along without them since they owned most of the marketplaces where my goods were sold.

I knowed that they were not giving me the best prices, but I only went to the markets that gave me the best I was gonna get, and I could live with that. There was still enough to give away to those in need and to take care of my family. I couldn't ask fo' much mo' than that.

It was near time fo' the boys to get back to their schooling, and James reminded me that they never got to see the music show I had promised them while we were heading home.

He saw a sign with writing on it. "There's another one this coming weekend," he said. "Could we go?"

Cleveland Jr. quickly began to agree with his brother that we had missed the other one.

"I know," I said, "I owes you that, and I'm sho that we should be able to make it iffin yo' mama says it's OK."

"Yeah," they both said at the same time, then broke out into song: "We going to the music show. We going to the music show."

I looked at the both of them and smiled.

Saturday came around quickly. The boys were excited that they were going to the music show. There was three country music groups playing. I parked the car in the colored section and looked to see where we were allowed to go to see the show. As it was, the colored section was way off from the center stage and in back of the white folks' section.

As the first group got to singing, I looked at the boys. They was a-stomping their feet and really enjoying the sound. 'Fo' long I was a-stomping myself. Even though I had never heard music like that befo', I was sure that I did kinda like it. It was not quite like the music I knew from church; it kinda lifted my sprit a bit the same way.

On the way home, I couldn't seem to get my mind offin the new-sounding music I had been introduced to, and I knew that the boys had had a good time.

"Papa, could we do this again when they come back?" Junior asked.

"We sho can," I answered quickly.

Summer harvest was in full swing. There was plenty of cotton to be picked, and the tomatoes and cucumbers were ready. I had added another three acres of cotton this season since last year we had done so good.

There were people coming in by the wagonload to work the fields. I had scales set up on each side of the field. I weighed on one side and Martha on the other. As the boys came home from school, they took over the scales as I paid the workers according to their loads. By the end of the day, I had full wagonloads ready fo' market and fo' the cotton gin mills.

The next morning, as the workers came in, I'd take the loads so's I could be back in time to man the scales again. This was the routine that seemed to work out the best, although there was times when work would come to a complete halt cause the rain would come; there just was no way to pick cotton when the rains came.

When the season was ending, I had two goats cooked overnight with all the fixings just as a way to thank the people who had worked so hard. We all took some time midday to come together over a meal. I said my thanks to them fo' their work. I could tell most of them liked the idea of the meal. I fo' sho liked the hard work they put in and the payoff it brought to me and my family. It was the least we could do to give back and say thanks to them all. Next season most would be happy to come back and do another harvest with us, and that was important fo' us to consider when we did these little things to show our appreciation.

PART III
CHAPTER 7

1948

Harlem, New York

It was a cold February morning. It had snowed a few days before, and the ground was quite slick as my mother made her way back home from visiting a friend up the street. We lived on 110th Street in a small house; the friend lived on 113th Street.

Mama was pregnant with me, and I was due to arrive any day—or to be clear, any minute. On February 27, at 3:45 a.m., mama woke with the pain that she knew quite well after having had my two sisters and two brothers. She was going into labor, and I didn't seem to want to give her time to get dressed and get to the hospital, which was several blocks away. My sister was told to get mama's friend to come over quickly; she would be able to help with the delivery.

I really don't know very much about my time in the house on 110th Street. As far as I was concerned, my life started on my fifth birthday. I remember my father had baked me a large cake. It had candles and icing, and he helped me blow out the candles. At that time, we lived on the Lower East Side of Manhattan. Me and my brother Jobie had to memorize the address before we were able to go outside to play. Mama said that if we ever got lost, we were to tell the police we lived at 10-17 FDR Drive, in apartment 3C.

It was later that year that I was able to go to a school, where I was able to play with other children that were not from the building that I lived in. I was OK with the friends I had there were white kids and Spanish kids and black kids. My best friends were Andrew, a black kid, and Bobby, a white kid. We always played together.

As I got older, other kids started to move into the building and the white kids moved out. I remember I asked Bobby why he was moving, and he didn't have an answer. I felt bad when he finally moved, but for some reason I didn't understand, almost all the white friends I had where starting to move from the area and more and more black and Spanish kids were moving in.

After a while the gangs started up in our project and the surrounding area. The gang in my area was the Sportsmen. They would fight with other gangs that were in the other projects, such as the Untouchables or the Dragons.

Mama told me and Jobie that we were never to join any gang. She said that it was a bad thing to do and that we would be punished if she ever found out that we had. We were instructed that we were to look out for our sisters Rosalind and Angela and that we needed to make sure that they, too, stayed away from gang members.

By the mid-1950s there had been many cases of gang members killing each other. Mama began to worry about our safety since it was mainly young boys that were being harmed. My father was a chef on a ship and was not home enough to look after us as he would if he had been there, so Mama began to send us away for the summer while we were out of school.

I kinda liked going away for the summer, until I began to realize that I was the one going more than anyone else. After a time, Mama would stop sending Jobie and she never sent Rosalind or Angela, but I still went. I, for the life of me, couldn't figure out why Mama was doing this to me. Over time the thought was beginning to set into my head that in fact she didn't love me like she did my brothers and sisters. I was a problem to her, so she had to get me away from her as much as she could.

It never occurred to me that Mama had told me not to be around the gang members in our area, and I kinda liked the excitement of being around them. Nor did it occur to me that I had taken my first drink and was brought home drunk after hanging out with those guys. Oh, not to mention I was running from the police, who knew every kid in the neighborhood by name and knew all the parents also. I just couldn't understand why mama didn't love me.

I was twelve years old, and there was excitement in the area. Someone was taking children while they played outside their homes, and they were being found dead. Mama became very upset about this. The police couldn't seem to catch this person.

School was about to end, and mama wanted me and Jobie out of the area. When she told us that we were going to stay with our grandfather on a farm, I only liked the idea that at least someone other than just me was going away. I thought that she wanted to protect Jobie and still get rid of me at the same time.

It was arranged: the day after school ended for the summer, Jobie and I would be on the Metro liner heading to South Carolina for a summer with my grandfather Cleveland. Mind you, I was eleven years old and by this time, I had a girlfriend named Linda. I for the life of me could not feel right going away for a whole summer and not being able to see my Linda, but it was set in stone. I was going.

I met with Linda later that day and told her the bad news. She said that she would be waiting for me to return, but I somehow didn't think that would be the case. I felt that this was the end of our relationship. When I got home and started packing—by now I was very good at packing—I cried. Jobie seemed to be enjoying this whole thing, even though I knew he had a girlfriend too. How do you leave a girlfriend?

The dreaded day came, and we grabbed our bags and headed out the door. I said my goodbyes to Rosalind and Angela just as I had several times before. Mae was there also. She, I'm sure, was glad to see me go as she wouldn't have to look after me; she was my oldest sister, and Mama used to have her take me with her when she went out from time to time. I could always tell that she didn't like that very much.

We took the bus to the subway and the subway to Grand Central Station, where we were to board the train for the long ride to South Carolina. Mama had packed us a bag with food in it; I knew that there were sandwiches, fruit, chicken, and cookies. Having done this type of thing many times before, I also knew that I had to ration my food so that it would last throughout the train ride. So of course I had to share some of my food with Jobie, who was done with his bag by the time morning came.

I looked out the window as the landscape went from towns to farms. There were rows and rows of items growing from the ground. Nowhere in New York City did I see this type of thing, although there was the time that I was sent to Upstate New York; there was some farmland there, but mostly there were trees, all kinds of trees, some with fruit and some with nuts. This, however, was different and something quite new to me. I tried to take it all in as I dealt with the pain I was feeling having to leave my Linda.

It was around eleven o'clock when the man came through the train car that Jobie and I were in. "Yemassee. Next stop Yemassee, South Carolina." The man came over to our seats and took the tickets that he had placed on the top of the seat earlier. "You two will be getting off at this stop," he said to Jobie. I was still looking out the window, this time at dusty roads and old houses and smaller farms. Now it was really sinking in I would have to spend the rest of the summer in a run-down shack on a dusty road.

As the train pulled into the station, we had already placed our bags where we could grab them and exit the train. Jobie grabbed the biggest one as he was the stronger of us; I was left to handle the littler one. When the train stopped, the man again called out the name "Yemassee, South Carolina" in a load voice. "All passengers getting off here come this way," he continued as he looked at Jobie and I. There might have been four other people getting off along with us; two got off first, then me, followed by Jobie, and the two other people.

I stepped away from the train and looked back for my brother. He was not very far behind, carrying the larger bag. As I turned back around to head toward where the other two people were going, a man walked up to me. He had dark skin and was wearing a floppy hat with a wide brim. He was dressed in overalls like I had only seen on TV, and his hatband was missing and replaced with a dark band of sweat. I quickly knew that this man was my grandfather. There was something about him: even though anyone could tell he had been beaten by the sun and hard work; he was calming to look at; his eyes were those of a man who took good care of his family.

"I'm yo' grandpa," he said to me in a gentle but stern voice as he reached for the suitcase I was carrying. I was still in awe of the sight of this man, how he stood up straight, shoulders back and chest out. I could tell even through the old clothes he was wearing that he was a strong man built from hard work.

He took my suitcase and walked over and spook to Jobie. Later Jobie would tell me of the time granddad came to our house for a visit when I was younger—that's where he remembered him from. We walked behind Granddad to a pickup truck. It was old and made a loud sound when it started. Our bags had been placed in the open back.

On the ride to his house, I kept looking back to see if our bags were still there. Some of the roads we were on were quite bumpy, and the bags would bounce up and down; I didn't want to lose my clothes on the way to the house. The truck windows were rolled down, and even with the wind made by the moving truck, it was hotter that I ever remembered it being at any time.

After what seemed to be forever, we turned off the highway and onto another dirt road. Off in the distance I could see the outline of a wooden house. I wondered if that was where we were going to end up, but it was off to the right and we turned left onto yet another dirt road.

On the first road, there were rows and rows of cotton. I had never seen raw cotton growing from a plant like that. Then, as we turned left on the other dirt road, there were rows of other crops to the left and a small stream to the right. Most of the area was covered by woods and trees of all types and sizes. Soon I could see the structure of a rather large house. As we drew nearer, I could see more details. The house was made of dark wood. There were three steps to the porch, which had a two-seater swing, a bench made of wood with a few pillows on it, and chairs scattered across the rest of its large area.

Granddad pulled the truck into a shed that was off to the right. "We're here," he said as he shut the noisy vehicle off.

I was in the middle, so I had to wait for Jobie to get out first. He stepped down and turned to tell me to watch my step jumping off the high step on the truck to the ground.

Granddad had already left the truck and was walking to the house with our bags in tow. I followed my brother as he made his way up the three stairs and onto the porch. As granddad reached the door, I could see the gray-haired woman looking out.

The woman opened the door and held it as we entered. She was a pretty woman; even at her age, you could see that. She was dressed in a long dress, and an apron was tied around her waist. I was hungry after the long ride and having to share my food with my brother and was delighted to smell the food coming from the kitchen.

"This is Ms. Ida," Granddad told us as we entered a large room.

She smiled and said hello to us individually, even asking our names as she did so. "I hope y'all are hungry," she said, then announced that she had made us a meal.

"I sure am," I quickly stated. Jobie just nodded his head in agreement.

From another section of the room, I could hear granddad calling my name. I followed the voice and entered into what was to be my room. The small suitcase was placed on the bed, which was made up with a patchwork quilt laid over it. With all the looking around I did, I didn't see where I was to go to the bathroom; I was sure it must be in one of the rooms I saw where the door was shut. I would be sure to ask where I could wash up.

There was not much to do other that to get to that good-smelling food, so I just opened my suitcase and found the closet space, where I'd be able to hang up my things later. I walked out of the room and back toward where we had come in when Ms. Ida called my name. I followed the direction of her voice into a large kitchen where the food was in pots on a stove unlike any I had ever seen. There were stacks of wood off to the right of the large stove, and I could see the fire burning underneath. I asked where I might be able to wash up and was told that there was water in the backyard in a pail for me. As I left the kitchen area, going toward the door to the backyard, I could see Jobie already washing up in the pail. He pointed me to one that I could use.

Something told me that I wasn't going to like having to go to the open space of a yard that also housed chickens to wash up. I could only imagine what it would be like to take a bath. Was this the place for that too? I wondered. Jobie was done, and I asked him if he had gone to the bathroom yet. He had not, he said, but he had asked and found out it was away from the house. Granddad was going to show it to us after we had dinner, he said. I surely didn't like the sound of that.

The meal was great: there was stewed chicken, cornbread, snap beans, and rice; for dessert there was peach cobbler. I was stuffed after all of that, yet Ms. Ida had already begun cooking another meal for later that evening.

There was no more time left; I had to use the bathroom. I asked granddad where it was, and he told me to follow him outside. We walked over a board that went over the small stream and up a slight incline. When we got there, I saw it was a small shack with a door that opened into a area with a wooden plank with two holes in it where you could sit down. This was where you went to the bathroom.

As I looked it over, I was pretty sure that this was not the safest place to come to at night or any other time, for that matter, and I was not sure if I could do this at all. By then granddad was heading back to the house, leaving me to my business. I used it that once but was going to ask for something else for the rest of my stay.

I made my way back to the house, monitoring my steps carefully: I was pretty sure that in a place like this, there were snakes and other dangerous animals that could cause me harm. I couldn't wait to tell Jobie about this situation. I wondered how he was going to handle it. No matter what, I wasn't going out there anymore, not me, not ever again, or so I thought. I found out quickly that the alternative was bad also.

When I got back to the house, there were other people there: two young women. Granddad told me that these were my aunties Martha and Alneata, whom we called Neat. I also noticed that the doors that were closed when we came in were now open. They were the rooms that my aunts stayed in. Both had just got back from school.

I wondered where Jobie was. I wanted to tell him about the place away from the house where the bathroom was. He was in the room he was given when we came in.

"Do you know where the bathroom is?" I said to him as I walked into his room.

"Yeah, he said, I had to go earlier."

"Were you afraid?" I asked, wanting him to agree that it was a risky place to get to with danger all around.

"Maybe what we'll have to do is go together," he said. "It might be safer that way."

"I don't know if I can go back there," I said.

"What else is there to do?" he asked.

"Granddad said that I could use a bucket in my room; I think I'd rather do that," I said.

"What happens to the bucket after you use it for a bathroom? It will end up staying in your room until you must take it and empty it, and where do you think you can empty it at?" Jobie asked. "Also, it will stink up your room, and that will bring in flies and who knows what. Just let me know when you must go, and I'll go with you."

"I think I'm gonna try the bucket first," I said. "If it becomes a problem, I'll have to change."

"Well, do what you have to do," Jobie said. "I think I can make it to the outhouse."

"Is that what they call it?" I asked.

"Yeah, that's what it is called," Jobie answered.

I left his room and returned to mine. In the middle of the floor was a large bucket.

I managed to make it through the night without using the bucket. I remembered that even if I were to use it—and I certainly didn't plan on giving it up—I would still have to clean it out. To me, that meant that I would still end up going to the outhouse.

I could see from my room window that Jobie was already up. He was using the bucket outside in the backyard. Ms. Ida was also up. I had seen her at the water well brining water into the house. There was also the smell of bacon coming from the kitchen. I didn't know what time it was; I had been awakened by the large chicken making loud choking sounds just a while earlier. I would come to know that sound every morning of my stay there.

I retrieved my pants and shirt from the chair I had left them on. I really needed to get to the outhouse, and Jobie was finishing up in the backyard. I was gonna take him up on the offer to walk with me. When I got to the kitchen, Ms. Ida was taking a pan filled with biscuits out of the oven with the wood fire burning underneath. Between the bacon and the biscuits, I was getting pretty hungry. I called out to Jobie to get his attention; he was watching the many chickens that were walking around the yard.

I shouted out to him until I got his attention. Ms. Ida was looking at me as though I had a problem. "Good morning, Ms. Ida," I said, realizing that I hadn't said that earlier. "How are you doing?"

"Good morning to you too," she said. "I'm doing just fine, and what are you making such a fuss about so early?"

"Aw, nothing. Just trying to get my brother's attention," I answered as Jobie was walking in the door. "Could you walk with me outside?" I asked, not wanting it to be known that I wanted him to walk me to the outhouse.

It wasn't very long before Jobie stopped walking me to the outhouse and I had to go on my own. He had gotten interested in the farm animals, riding the goats and messing with the pigs. I was trying to erase my fear of all those animals, but for some reason I liked riding the mule. That should have bothered me more because of how high up in the air I was while riding.

I also got to know more about all the land that my grandfather owned. Martha walked me around on the days she was not attending school. I found out that the patch of land on the way to the house with the cotton and corn and watermelon all belonged to granddad. She also told me that there was much more land, including the wooded area, as far as I could see, which he also owned.

I was thankful for Martha taking time with me like that. My other auntie, Neat, was very nice also, but she spent a good deal of time with her studies, and when she wasn't doing that, she too would join us for walks around the farm. I mostly got to sit and talk with granddad after supper. He got up before I did and was usually out in the fields by the time I was up and about.

My brother had by now learned some things about the farm that he would share with me while Martha and Neat were at school; he told me where he had seen a snake or about a pond he had discovered with fish swimming around in it. All these things only made me even more afraid than I was before he showed them to me. I came to realize that he was just trying to keep me from going into places that might hold danger for me. After all isn't that what big brothers are for?

The pond with the fish was also a place where black snakes would be, and a bite from one of them could cost you your life if not treated in time—I was glad to know that.

By summer's end I had become well versed with the farm way of life; I even took a shot at riding the goat and was thrown off quickly. Everything we needed was pretty much right there, so we didn't get to go to town for anything. There was church, and though I thought going to church on Sunday was a lot, sometimes we'd also ride for hours to get to church on other days when someone granddad liked was singing. That was not all bad: some of the groups were really very good, and we'd leave feeling good about having heard them sing.

There were the things I really missed, like Linda and television. Granddad didn't have a TV, and I missed the programs we used to watch, and the game shows Mama would use to play with us. I also missed my friends, so I was looking forward to getting back home. I wasn't sure if I was gonna tell anyone that I had to use an outdoor bathroom, nor was I gonna talk about trying to ride a goat and getting thrown from it, but I would mention being able to go into the field and pick out a watermelon. I'd also tell of being able to go to the henhouse and getting enough eggs for breakfast and chasing the pigs in the pigpen and coming up dirty as the pigs always outran me.

Yeah, there were some good stories to tell from this trip, along with some that would never be spoken out of my mouth. My brother was ready to get back to city life as well, even though he had been able to go places and do things I wasn't able to do. He would tell me about the stores in town where there were signs stating that white people could go in but he could not. I didn't understand why that was since where we lived, we were able to go into any of the stores; in fact, the store owners knew us by name and would speak to us when we came in. He also said that there were signs on water fountains that read *Whites Only* and even if he was thirsty, he couldn't drink.

I started to think that he was telling me that because he didn't want me to feel bad about not being able to go out with him and the older kids. I just couldn't believe that there could be such signs; it just didn't seem real.

The day before we were to go home, Ms. Ida cooked a big meal for us. She even baked a blueberry pie, and I just loved her blueberry pie. Jobie loved her peach cobbler, and she told him that there would be some for us to eat on the train ride home. I was glad that she had made the pie now because I wouldn't have wanted to wait until the next day for it.

That night we all sat around on the porch. Some of the older kids came to say their goodbyes, mostly to Jobie. Martha and Neat exchanged greetings on having had this time to get to know us. I think it was then that I wished for a moment that we had more time—both had been so nice to us, but our time there was up.

By now I was used to the rooster crowing at sunup. In fact, I really didn't get very much sleep, so I was awake when he began his ritual. I could smell the bacon and other aromas coming from the kitchen. I looked out the window, wondering if Jobie was already up. If so, he would be washing up in the backyard. There was no one there but the chickens. There had been some hatchlings too, and they were running around behind one of the larger chickens.

I got up, put on a pair of pants and a shirt, and went to the kitchen. "Good morning, Ms. Ida," I announced.

"Good morning, Al," she answered as she continued to stir the contents of the cast-iron pan that was on the stove. "Are you happy ta be goin' home?"

"Yeah," I said quickly, then thought maybe I shouldn't have done so. "I think so."

I went into the yard to the pail of water that was there to wash up with. I washed my face and hands and dried with the towel on the side of the small table; this was the usual way in the morning, except when we wanted to take a bath. For a bath we would use the large washbasin and fill it with water in the morning and let it sit in the sun for an hour or so, add some hot water from the stove, and when it was right, get in and take our bath.

We didn't have to leave for some time, and I saw that there were two large washbasins with water in them off to the side of the house. I came into the house still wondering where Jobie was since I could see that his door was open. I asked Ms. Ida if she knew.

"I saw him heading out front," she answered. "Don't know much where he went, though."

"I'll go take a look," I said.

"Y'all come back and have some breakfast," she said.

"Yes, we sure will," I said, knowing that I, for one, was hungry and those smells were only making me more so.

As I walked out the screen door to the front porch, I could see Jobie sitting on the swing. He was just looking out at the trees and the rows of corn planted near the house. There was a hummingbird flying nearby; I had never seen a hummingbird before coming to the farm, and this one had greeted me many a morning.

"Ms. Ida wants us to come into breakfast," I said. "Are you OK?"

"Yeah, just getting some last looks," he answered. "There's nothing like this back home."

"Yeah, I know what you mean. I'm gonna miss this too," I said as I sat beside him.

The time seemed to go by quickly. Granddad came into my room to pick up my suitcase. I had packed the night before, and of course I left some room for whatever Jobie was not going to be able to get in his suitcase.

"Are you ready?" granddad asked.

"Yes, Grandpa, I'm ready," I answered somewhat reluctantly, still wondering if Jobie was going to need some space in my suitcase for something.

"Well, let's get ta getting," he said while reaching for my bag. "Yo' brother is waiting outside fo' us on the porch."

I followed him out of the room, then realized that I hadn't said goodbye to Ms. Ida. We had said our goodbyes to Martha and Neat the night before because we knew that we weren't going to see them this morning. "I'm going to go to the kitchen and say goodbye to Ms. Ida," I said.

"You won't have to do that," he said. "She's on the porch waiting fo' you."

Granddad took the bag to the pickup truck, and I turned to say goodbye to Ms. Ida. "I had a good time," I told her, and I thanked her for all the really good cooking and being so nice to me. She had the usual smile on her face as she handed me a brown paper bag from which I could smell the butter cake that I liked so much.

"Thank you for coming," she said as she handed me the paper bag. "It was nice getting to know you."

I took the bag from her hand and gave her a hug. I wasn't sure if it was OK to do that; I just wanted to do it, so I did. I wasn't sure, but I think she had a tear in her eye when I released her from my grip. "Goodbye," I said, then made my way down the three steps and toward the waiting truck; it seemed that I was the holdup.

Jobie was waiting for me at the passenger side of the truck. I was to sit in the middle and he at the window. I took my place, and we were off to the train station. I looked at the land again, this time having a better understanding that it was my granddad's. I was still amazed at just how much there was of it. A farm—a whole big farm, I said to myself. This was something I'd be talking about to my friends for some time.

The ride to get back to the station didn't seem to take as long as it had coming. We pulled into a section that had a sign saying *Colored Parking*. I realized that I hadn't seen that before, even though we had come this way to get to the truck when we arrived.

Granddad took our bags from the back of the truck and walked us into the outside waiting area, where there was another black woman, and a black man seated under a canopy. It wasn't long before I spotted the water fountain with the sign on it: *Whites Only*.

This is what Jobie was talking about, I thought to myself as I took it all in. Over to the right was a station house

I noticed three white folks going into; they didn't come out until the train came. I was confused since where we lived, everybody was able to sit where they wanted. And at all the water fountains I'd stopped at to get a drink of water in the parks and other areas in New York, there were no signs like the ones I'd seen here.

I couldn't seem to get what I saw out of my mind. Throughout the entire train ride home, I was thinking about what all of that was about and why it was that way there and not that way where I lived. That would bother me for a short while as I'd find out that it did exist even in New York City; it was just done differently, not so open in terms of water fountains or where you could sit.

CHAPTER 8

1960

I was a bit excited I was going to another school this year. I had heard about it, and some said that it was filled with gangs. Growing up on the Lower East Side of Manhattan, we were somewhat used to gangs, as I've mentioned: the Sportsman was the gang in my project, and just up the street there were the Dragons and the Untouchables, so I did know something about the gangs, but my brother had kept me away from all of that. Now I was going to be in a school where they all came together and Jobie, though he would be there the first year, wouldn't be around me much or able to send me home if things got a little out of hand.

I wasn't afraid of fighting. I did my share of that even in my project, and I was pretty good with my hands, as they say, but there was no way to win when you had to fight a gang of kids all at once. I wasn't sure just how I would handle something like that; I never had to before. Jobie did say that all I really needed to do was stay away from the gangs and mind my business. I was sure that I could do that, but I heard that they would take kids' lunch money and clothing, and I wasn't sure that I would be able to take that. Jobie said that if I had to fight, I should just fight as hard as I could and not give up or give in to anyone trying to bully me.

PS 60 was also a longer distance away from home than where I had been going to school, and some of the route was through the other gangs' territories. That in and of itself could cause problems in just getting to school or getting home from school. Others in my project had made it through, and now it was my turn to see if I could as well. I had heard that Linda was also going to be there, though she never did wait for me. When I got back home from my farm visit, I was told by my fried that she was seeing another guy.

My first week of school went well. I realized that I had friends from my old school, so we quickly connected with each other. You know the saying, "safety in numbers." There was a guy who stared at me a lot, and that was usually not a good sign in the projects. Whenever someone did that to you, it was a call to question why it was happening. I remembered what Jobie said: I was to not start anything, just not let anyone put their hands on me. This fell in that category; since it was just a stare, I would wait for whatever was going to happen to happen.

It took another two weeks before it played itself out when he came over to me and bumped me hard. I nearly fell to the ground, but didn't as he turned to take a swing at me. I jumped back and got into my fighting stance. It was on. I quickly realized that he didn't have the boxing skills that I had after he threw a few punches, so I set him up with some jabs before knocking him to the ground. I could have listened to the crowd that had formed and got on top of him while he was down, but I choose not to. Instead, I allowed him to get to his feet. I could tell that he didn't want anything else to do with fighting me, but the crowd had gotten to him with their shouts. I punched him around some more this time, not wanting to hurt him badly; it was enough to let him know that he was not going to win a fight that day. I knocked him down again, then asked if it was over. He said it was. I had no further trouble with fighting at PS 60 for the next few years.

My grades were pretty good, and I found something I really liked doing when I was chosen to act in the school's play. I don't know what it was that made me try out for the play; I probably wanted to impress some girl in one of my classes and thought this might be a good way to do so. At any rate, I was good, and I really enjoyed doing it.

Though the play was a good thing, the gang situation was getting worse. It was at the point where I was being sought after. My reputation was getting stronger as I became a familiar boxer at the local Boys Club.

I was setting my sights on becoming a professional boxer but as a mama's boy didn't like the fact that she would not come to see me at any of my fights. I asked her several times to come and see how good I was, but she never did. One day I just outright asked her why, and her reply was "I'll never come to see someone hitting my child." That wrapped up my boxing-for-a-living idea. I didn't want to do anything that she would not want to come and see me do, so when I wasn't acting, I was in the band.

I, too, was getting pretty wrapped up in how the gang leader was giving me the business about how cool it would be being a member. He said that I was a good fit 'because I had guts and could fight. I felt kinda special.

One day I went to the meeting. It was held in the FDR Park. I was surprised to see so many of my friends there. Some I had wondered what had happened to since I wasn't seeing them at the Boys Club or participating in any of the area ball teams that they used to be a part of. The meeting was about going to another project and jumping some of their gang members who had beaten up one of our guys. Several of the members had chains, the kind you would use to tie your bike to a fence, others had switchblade knives, and some had baseball bats. As I looked around at this crowd of guys and began to understand their intent, I became worried. I wondered just how I was going to get out of this mess I was in. As I tried to figure out what I was going to do, I heard a familiar voice. It was Jobie, and he was calling me.

"Hey guys, I gotta go," I said as I walked toward my brother's voice. Once again, he had shown up in time.

Jobie had his own reputation. I'm not sure of just how he got it: I never saw him fight anyone, nor did I see him in a confrontation with anyone, but from what I know about getting a rep, he must have done something that gave him that kind of clout in the projects. No one wanted any trouble with him, and that made it possible for him to walk right into situations I might get myself into without any challenge from anyone. That was good and sometimes not so good, like the time I wanted to fight this kid, and we agreed to meet after school in the park on Tenth Street. I was there and raring to go when a guy I didn't even know told the guy I was getting ready to fight that I was Jobie's brother. Suddenly, the guy was telling me he was going to give me a break and not fight me. Heck, I wanted to fight him, but now I wasn't going to get the chance. For the most part, it was good having a brother like Joe. He saved my butt more times than I could count, and that was needed given the kind of trouble I would have gotten into.

Over the course of just a few months, some of these guys I remembered from the gang meeting were dead. Two were killed in gang-related violence, one was killed attempting to rob a store, and one was on his way to jail for murder. I was glad that I didn't get involved with them and thankful for my brother.

The neighborhood was still getting worse. Every summer, right after school was out, I was sent away. There was the Privet home in Upstate New York. The white family would meet me at the train, and I would spend the summer with them and their daughter. It was always fun. I went there two years and really enjoyed the time out of the city.

Then came my last year in junior high school, and I had to choose a high school to go to. Two of my best friends were killed just moments after I left them. I'm not sure, but I think that sealed my fate for the summer and beyond: I was leaving.

It was three days before school was out for the summer when Mama told me to begin packing. She said that I was going away, and she left my room. I didn't think much about it since I usually went away for the summer anyway and I did like going upstate to be with the family there. The whole town kinda got to know me, and everyone was so nice to me. I liked them too and was getting excited about going back there—we went boating and camping and did all sorts of good stuff.

The day arrived, and Jobie came in to help me with my bag. That was a bit different, but what the heck, if he didn't carry it, I would have to, so I didn't mind so much that he came and took it out for me. The bus and train rides were also a bit different. No one was talking. By this time Mama typically would have gone over the dos and don'ts and reminded me that I was to be on my best behavior while away from home. It wasn't until we got to Grand Central Station that I realized that this was a different trip I was going on. We were in another part of the station than we were in when I went upstate. Mama handed me my ticket, and I read the destination: Yemasee, South Carolina. I was going back to Granddad's farm, and Jobie wasn't going with me this time.

Mama hugged me and said goodbye, then turned away quickly. Jobie walked me on the train and to my seat, where he put my bags away.

"You take care of yourself," he said as he began to leave the train. He handed me a bag with some sandwiches and a drink. He didn't look back, so he didn't see that I was crying. I looked out the window and saw Jobie waving.

I'm not sure, but I think he was crying too; although I couldn't swear on it, I'm pretty sure that he was. Mama kept her head down so I couldn't tell whether she was OK, but she did have a hankie in her hand, and I saw her wipe her eyes once or twice. Maybe she, too, was crying; I just don't know. But I sure was.

I cried myself out, and the realization came I was gonna be away for the whole summer and there just wasn't anything I could do about that. There still was something wrong, and I couldn't quite put my finger on it. This was so very different from when I left home the other times. I just couldn't figure out what it was. Then I remembered that when I looked at my ticket, there was no return trip. That was it: I always knew when I was going home. I looked at the ticket again. I was right. There was no return date on it, and we hadn't had our usual talk about being back in time for school clothes shopping.

I wanted to not think about it, but I couldn't seem to get it out of my mind: When will I be going home? That was the question I kept asking myself. Why don't I have a return ticket back to New York? I was becoming desperate for an answer, and there was nobody to ask. Surely my grandfather would know the answer, and I was going to ask him as soon as I got off the train.

It was a restless night, and I didn't get much sleep, nor did I eat the sandwiches I had in my bag until what must have been two or three in the morning, after which I finally went to sleep. When I woke, the sun was up and I could see the country zooming by from my seat. I remembered when I saw this before, it was a sight to behold, and then I was not alone heading so far away from home and not knowing for how long.

The conductor had called out the next stop, which was in North Carolina. I knew that I was going to South Carolina, which meant that I was going to be on this train for a bit more time. I made my way to the bathroom at the end on the train car; I was able to wash my face and hands there. I got back to my seat and fetched the last sandwich from the bag. There was also half a container of fruit juice and a Hostess cupcake. This would be my meal until I got to Granddad's house, so I ate it slowly.

I wondered if Ms. Ida was still there and if she would be making a big meal for me for when I got there. I wondered if by now there was a bathroom inside the house so I wouldn't have to use that out house again. I had so many questions, and there were so many improvements I could only wish had been made to the house for my comfort.

As I looked out the window, I could see my reflection looking back at me. There was a look I had never seem before in myself; it was a look of despair and uncertainty. I wondered for a moment if I was afraid. I remembered being uncertain as to why Mama always sent me away.

I remembered feeling that she didn't want me around so she sent me away from her, but usually I would get over that when I would come home, and she and I would spend time shopping for school clothes, or she'd take me to the different ventures I'd gotten myself into. Those times seemed to make up for the pain I would feel in leaving home, and there were all the good places I would go for the summer and the fun things I would get to do while away, but this was different: there was no sign of when I'd return to those times me and Mama had.

The thought came that I might never see Mama again, and that was the hardest thing for me to bear. I was sad, truly sad, and I never remembered it being this bad before, never. I wanted to cry, but the tears just wouldn't come. If this is what it has come to, if I finally have to face life without Mama, then so be it, I thought. I had to be strong even if just for little bits at a time; this is not gonna break me. I finished my meal and dozed off. This time was different; I slept until I heard the announcement by the conductor. "Yemasee," he said in a strong voice. "Next stop is Yemasee, South Carolina."

This is where I get off, I said to myself. This is my new life.

The conductor placed my suitcase at the exit door where the colored people got off the train. I was not sure as to how I was going to fare getting it off the train since

Jobie put it on the train for me. As the train stopped, I was relieved as the neatly suited black man reached up and brought the suitcase to the ground. Grandpa was there to pick it up from where the suited man had put it.

Although I remembered him from my visit three years ago, he did look a bit changed. The hat with the big rim was there, as was the sweatband, but there was something about his face—it was as if he had aged ten years to my three. He greeted me with a hello and asked if my trip was a good one. I wanted to say that I cried all night, and I didn't understand why I was being punished by having to come here for the rest of my life, but I choose to just say the trip was OK.

I followed him to the exit where black folk were gathering and loading and unloading bags from their cars and trucks. I looked for the pickup truck that he had used the last time I was there but could not find it among the few cars and trucks that were in that area. Grandpa walked over to a blue car and opened the trunk with a key. He placed my suitcase in the trunk and closed it, then opened the door for me to get in and walked around the other side, where he sat behind this very large wheel with a bar attached. He put the key into a slot, and the car came to life with a loud engine sound.

Within minutes we were heading out of the area. This was not the first time I had been in a car. In fact, I had been in cars throughout my young life, but I had never seen one with the steering wheel so big or with the stick that he would move from one position to another as we drove along.

I was fascinated just looking at him as he pushed the stick up, then pulled the stick down, then pushed it up again. I watched him until he stopped moving the stick at all and we were driving at a good speed. I wondered if I could learn how to drive a car like that. There was so much going on, but he made it seem easy. That became something to ponder since I was going to be with him for the rest of my life. There's probably going to be many things that this man is gong to get to teach me as I grow up, and I need to accept that starting right now, I thought.

The ride to the house didn't seem as long as I remembered it from the last time I was there; in fact, it seemed quite short. This time I knew when we came across his land after the turn onto the dirt road. I could see the lines of crops perfectly standing as if they were at attention. From field to field, there were different sizes and shapes of growth as far as I could see. I didn't know just what it was that was planted in those fields, but I knew that my grandpa was responsible for it being there.

As we drove toward the house, I scanned to see if the outhouse was still there; that was one of my pet peeves about this place. Another was the fact that there was no electricity in the house when I was there before. I hoped the latter was fixed since I did see telephone poles and electric poles where there were none before.

As we turned onto the road directly to the house, I could see the outhouse. Maybe he just didn't tear it down, I said to my self, hoping that I was right and there was both a bathroom and electricity in the house. Grandpa parked the car off to the side of the house, and we got out. I could see Ms. Ida standing in the doorway. She was a lovely woman and hadn't changed a bit, wearing her apron and long dress and a smile. I was glad to see her and quickly thought about her good cooking.

Grandpa took my bag out of the trunk and walked up the steps to the house. He greeted Ms. Ida and went inside. I stopped to greet Ms. Ida also but thought to give her a hug as well. Her smile got much wider as I gave her that hug, and she welcomed me back. I followed Granddad into the house, and the first thing I noticed was a big TV off to the side. I realized that there were also lights on in the kitchen area, and Granddad motioned me to my room, which also had electric lights. Now all I needed for him to do was show me where the bathroom was since I was ready to go. No one mentioned it, so I asked, "Where's the bathroom?"

"It's where its aways been," grandpa said. "You just go outside and over the stream down to the outhouse."

"Hurry back," Ms. Ida said. "I cooked something nice for you—you must be hungry by now."

I made my way to the outhouse and back as quickly as I could, then made my way to the backyard where the washbasins where and washed my face and hands. Passing through the kitchen, I could smell the fried chicken and corn bread. I rushed to my place at the table. Grandpa said grace, and we ate a great meal.

I remembered from before that there was not a lot of talking at the dinner table, but when we were done and Grandpa went out to the front porch to smoke, I followed; I had so many questions I wanted answers to. I took my seat on the swing next to where he sat on the wooden chair.

"Where are Neat and Marsha?" I asked, not knowing why I led with that.

"Oh, they moved out," he said. "There ain't nobody but me and Ida been here fo' a time."

I wanted to turn the questions to myself and how I felt about being here, but somehow that didn't seem to be appropriate at this time. Maybe they just need me there.

A little over a week had passed. I was attempting to forget how homesick I was, but each day I would spend some time thinking about home. I was becoming more at ease with being there, although I tried to fight it. Ms. Ida was just the sweetest woman and would ask me what

I liked to eat so that she could be sure to make it for me. Grandpa had his routine where he would get up before the sun rose, roll himself two packs of cigarettes, have breakfast, and head out to the fields.

The rooster would wake me most of the time, but in the first few days, I just couldn't get enough sleep, so I'd hear grandpa and Miss Ida in the kitchen. Twice I got up, which was how I got to see what grandpa was doing.

In the day I would help to feed the pigs and the chickens. The pigpen was off to the left of the backyard, and the chickens were in the backyard. I kinda liked having those things to do. I especially liked that the pigs and the chickens came around when they saw me coming. At times I would act as if I was gonna go another way, and they would follow me until I threw the corn to the chickens or poured the mixture into the pigs' bins. I'd stand there and watch the animals as they ate what I brought for them.

It was around the middle of the fourth week when I became ill. My entire body was broken out in puss-filled bumps. I would try to walk from my bedroom to the kitchen and would black out. I would come to in my bed, where it was hard for me to want to stay because these bumps would pop open, and I'd be lying in the wetness.

Grandpa knew what was wrong with me. He said that I had chicken pox, and he would rub me with a paste-like lotion. I tried hard to be strong as he would rub the paste over the bumps on my skin, but most of the time, I would cry out in pain and again black out.

Grandpa looked after me with such care. He fed me and sat with me. I don't remember a time when I awoke that he wasn't sitting there either with a cold cloth or the salve that he applied to my skin until I was able to stand without falling and bumps were nothing more than spots on my skin. From then on I had a different feel about my grandpa. I felt something that drew me closer to him. I felt his love.

It would be a few more days before I was feeling completely well again. Ms. Ida cooked some of my favorite foods, and I was back to eating good again. grandpa was back to tending the fields, and I had my chores to do as well. One day I saw that he was loading up the pickup truck with some fruit he was taking into town; I asked if I could come along since I had completed all my chores. He looked at me for what seemed a very long time before agreeing to let me make the trip with him.

We drove for a few minutes in silence before he finally spoke. "Afo' we get to town, there is something ya needs ta know," he said. "You's gonna stay right by me. Don't go walking off. There are places in town they don't want you to go, and iffin you needs some water, tell me befo' you going drinking outta them folks' fountains. Iffin a white man asks you something, look him in the eye and answer just what he asks ya; don't go saying mo' than that 'cuz dey really don't want to talk to ya dey just want to know what dey ask. Now does ya understand?" he asked while still looking at the road ahead.

"I think so," I answered, knowing that none of what he said made any sense to me. I'd talked to white people many times and even asked them questions if I wanted to; this, to me, sounded like I had to be different toward them suddenly.

"You just do what I say, and we'll be OK," he continued. This time he turned his head toward me to see if I was really paying attention.

Grandpa pulled the truck into a space behind what to me looked like one of the grocery stores in my old neighborhood. I wondered why we were going behind the store when the door in the front was open. Grandpa got out and greeted a white man who come out as we pulled in. The man looked over the fruit in the back of the truck, then called out to two black men who were off to the side of the store.

"Y'all boys get me ten of them melons, a case of them berries, and two cases of them pecans. Put them the back room," he yelled out to the men. "I'll be right out to settle with ya," the white man continued as Grandpa watched the two men unload the items from the back of the pickup. I stayed in my seat, which was what grandpa had asked me to do.

The white man came back from inside the store and handed Grandpa some money; Grandpa checked the amount and put the bills into his wallet. The white man then came over to where I was seated in the car. "You's Cleveland's grandson?" he asked, looking at me.

I remembered what Grandpa had said and answered quickly, "Yep."

The white man walked back into the store, where the two black men had taken the last two items, and grandpa came back into the pickup truck. "Did well, son," he said as we drove off.

There would be six more stops, all pretty much the same: we would go around back, and some white man—and in one case, a white woman—would come out and look the items over, then have a black person come and take them off the truck. grandpa would get paid for the items and put the money in his wallet, and we'd move on.

We were ready to head home when I had to go to the bathroom. I mentioned to grandpa that I needed to go, and he asked me to hold on for a few minutes. He said that there was a place that I could use but it was not in that area.

We drove for what seemed quite a long time before grandpa pulled into a store that was not as nice as the ones we had seen in town. He motioned me to go around the side of the building where there was a door; as I opened it, I could see that it was an outhouse. At that point I only wanted to go I didn't matter where I went as long as I could relieve myself.

When we got back to the house, there was only a case of nuts left in the pickup. grandpa told me to go to the backyard and wash up. As I came through the house, I could smell the scent of the baked bread and other food coming from the kitchen. Ms. Ida was sitting at the table greasing a large yam. She was humming a song I remembered from church but didn't know the words to. I stopped to say hello to her, and she looked up at me with that large smile she always had for me.

"How'd it go?" she asked.

"I didn't understand some of what grandpa said to me, but I did what he said, so I guess it went pretty good," I answered.

"Well, you just do what he tells you when you're in town 'cuz he knows best 'bout those things since he has to deal with them folks," she said.

"But I don't understand how it could be so different here than where I live, in New York."

"It is, she said. "You need to know that it is very different, so always do what yo' grandpa say you should do, and you'll be all right. Now go wash up. I made something nice for you for after dinner."

I rushed out the back door and off to the table by the well where the pail of water that had been heated by the sunlight was. I wondered just what it could be that Ms. Ida had made for me. She was such a good cook, and she made ten or more dishes that I really liked a lot. I tried my sense of smell to figure out which one it was.

Dinner was good as always: pork chops, butter beans, corn bread, and rice. I ate more quickly then usual; I wanted to get at the surprise after dinner. Grandpa looked at how I was eating and said that I should slow down and chew my food. He joked that I was eating like them hogs out in the pen. I tried to slow down so that he wouldn't make fun of me, but it was hard to do. When I finished the food on my plate, I looked over the table at Ms. Ida. She, too, was laughing at me as she got up from the table and walked over to the window box where she sometimes kept cakes and pies. My eyes opened wide as she brought out the cherry pie. She made the best cherry pie I had ever tasted, and I held up my plate to receive my slice. It was better than I imagined.

The next weeks went by quickly. I went into town again with grandpa, and I was beginning to get good at the instructions I had been given, except that time when the white store owner called out, "Boy, come here and see this" and I began to move in the direction of his voice but shortly realized that he was talking to my grandpa. Grandpa looked at me and motioned me back to the pickup, then went to see what the white man was fussing about. I got into the pickup while listening to what was being said outside. The white man was complaining about some strawberries that had come out of the case. Grandpa said a few words to the white man and put the case of berries back on the truck. I could see out the side mirror the white man handing grandpa the money and grandpa putting it in the wallet with the money he had collected earlier. As we drove off, grandpa looked at me. I was still confused by the man calling grandpa boy, but it didn't seem to faze grandpa at all. I was wondering if I should ask about it or not when grandpa began to speak.

"See now dat's just the kinda thing you may have to go through wit' dees white folk. Dey talks ta ya any kinda ways sometime; it becomes up to you whether you let it bother you or conduct yo' business. I still got that white man's money in my pocketbook. Now I coulda done different, and who knows what might have happened. So, the lesson is, which would you want to do?"

"But he called you boy, and I was the only boy that was there," I said.

"It don't matter what he called me," Grandpa said. "It's the outcome that really matters, and I have the money in my pocket and a case of berries to give away."

There was a slight smile on grandpa's face, and somehow it kinda made me feel a little better about it even though I had never seen a grown-up called boy before.

We went to the store on the way out of town, the one with the outhouse. Grandpa stopped and called out to the men sitting outside in the front. "Take the case of berries," he said to one of the men who got up to greet him. The man took the case of strawberries into the small store. An older man came out and over to speak to grandpa.

"How much you want fo' them berries?" he asked.

"Nothing," grandpa answered. "Y'all just enjoy them."

"Well, I sures thanks ya," the man said and tipped his wide-brim hat.

We drove off again, and I could see a slight smile on grandpa's face. We listened to country music for the rest of the drive home. It was a good day.

CHAPTER 9

It was getting time to start school. By now I knew that I wasn't going back to New York and that I'd be going to the school in town. I received a letter from mama, and in it she sent some money for me to buy some new clothes. I really didn't need very much 'cause the only time I got to wear the nice clothes I had was church on Sunday, and right after getting back home, I'd take them off and put on my older clothes.

There where those times when we'd go to church on weekdays, but that was usually to hear a group or two that Grandpa really liked and wanted to see bad enough to drive for hours just to get to see in person. I enjoyed that too. Usually, it was the groups that we'd seen on TV and heard were going to be at a certain church during the week. Grandpa would say to Ms. Ida, "We's gonna go see them, so fix an early supper."

I got up early that Saturday morning; it was the day we planned to go into town and shop for something new for school. I used to love doing this with Mama. She and I would go from store to store usually because I was so picky about what I wanted to wear on the first day of school. I somehow knew that this was not going to be anything like what me and Mama did.

Grandpa was up and sitting at the dinner table rolling his cigarettes. Ms. Ida was taking a pan of cracklin' bread over to the counter near the wood stove. I could smell the bacon frying in the black pan.

"Good morning," I said as I made my way out to the backyard. I could hear both saying good morning to me even though I had left the kitchen area.

It was early, yet the yard was bustling with chickens and the birds that came down to feed with them—they seemed to know just when to enter the yard.

I made my way over to the bench where the pails and a pot of hot water were, being careful not to step on the many chickens running around the yard.

This was going to be my first day of school, and I had the jitters about what it was going to be like. I was told that I was to wait at the edge of the road for my ride to the new school. In New York, you took public transportation to school or on a good day, you just walked the ten or so blocks. My school was in another town, one I had been to a few times and where I was not able to enter the stores. I could only wonder what the school was gonna be like.

After breakfast I made my way to the place where I was to catch the bus to school; I was surprised to see a big yellow bus pull up to where I was standing. The door opened, and the young driver motioned for me to step in. I looked around and saw that all the cars on the roadway were stopped. I soon realized that they were waiting for me to get in the bus and for the bus to remove the stop sign. As I looked for a seat, I realized that there were only black kids around my age on the bus. That, too, was so different from New York City, where the bus would have all types of people.

I found a seat and was happy to be sitting next to a pretty light-skinned girl. I quickly attempted to introduce myself, only to be stopped by her announcing that she knew I was Mr. Golden's grandson James. She said that everyone on the bus had that information, then she said that her name was Allyson Greene. She then said, "It's nice to finally meet you, James Golden."

We talked through the rest of the ride to school, and I felt relieved that there were people my age that I could get to know and hang out with.

When the bus arrived at its destination and pulled in behind other buses, I glanced at the structure that would be my school. The big sign in front read Jasper High School. There were students and teachers gathered in various sections of the well-kept lawn. I had no idea where I was to go, so I followed Allyson to where she and some of the others on my bus had gathered.

The reality was quite clear that there were going to be no white people in this school; for as far as I could see, there was nothing but black students and black teachers. It wasn't long before I heard my name called, along with two other names. I stepped out of line and went over to the black woman that had called my name. She was a pretty brown-skinned woman with shiny black hair. She motioned me to stand by her side as she called out two other names. I was not sure of what to make of this, except that every student in the school got to see me standing by this woman. Before long the other students where heading for the school doors and we were walking through the side door and into a small office.

We were given some instructions on school policy and provided with a small map to carry in our pocket so that we could locate our classes. There were five buildings where classes were held, and there was a larger building where the gym and swimming pool were. We were given a grand tour of each of the buildings and shown where all the exits and entrances were before being taken to what would be our homerooms. One of the others called out was older than me and, in a grade, or two ahead of me. The other was my age and in the same grade; his name was Clarence, and he would become my good friend. Our homeroom teacher was Mrs. Bolton; she was a well-built woman who looked as if she could take down the average student with little to no real effort. She was also an English teacher whose class everyone really enjoyed being in.

The first day went well. Most of it was spent in our homeroom, where we were assigned lockers and given our schedule for the semester. We were also shown where we were to go in case of a fire and given general instructions on school practices and after-school activities. I was pleased to learn that there was something going on in and around the school both day and night. In New York City, you were sometimes able to take an arts-and-crafts course after school, but this was much different. Here you could do extra classwork with your teacher, prepare for tests with other students, do special projects for extra credit, see the home team play basketball or other sports events. What I liked the most, though, was the Saturday night dances.

I sat next to Allyson on the way back home, and she asked me what I thought of school. Of course she had to say it in a mocking way: "How'd you like our little school, compared to the big New York City schools you're used to?"

"I think this is about the finest school I've ever been in," I replied. "New York schools are big and all, but that only means you have to do a lot more walking to get to everything, and that makes it easier to get to class late, and who wants to get to class late?" I said.

"Oh, you're just saying that" she said.

"No, I really mean it," I said. "Cross my heart and hope to die."

We both laughed. We talked some more until my stop came. "See you tomorrow," I said as I excited the bus.

I think I'm gonna like it here, I said to myself for the first time. It wasn't that grandpa was in any way bad to be around and certainly not that Ms. Ida wasn't just about the best cook ever; it was just that now I had some people to talk to that were my age and there, too, was the possibility of a girlfriend in the mix. Yep, things are good, I thought.

As I headed down the road toward my grandfather's house, lifted by my newfound friend and the excitement of my new school, I heard my grandfather's voice. He was in the field about halfway up a plowed row. It was planting season, and he was in the middle of getting the field ready. I waved to him and came closer to where he would end up as he came down the field.

"How was yo' day?" Grandpa asked as he looked me in the eyes.

"It was really good," I answered, not wanting to seem too excited even though I was.

"Good," he said. He turned the mule around to begin plowing the next row. "I thought you'd be happy ta git round people yo' own age."

Now I felt bad that I had held back my excitement since even grandpa knew it would be a good thing for me. "It was great, grandpa," I said, adding a big smile. "I had a good day."

"Git on ta the house," he said. "Ida done fixed ya something to eat. We'll talk later."

"OK, Grandpa," I said as I began walking toward the house. I didn't get very far before I could smell the fresh-baked blueberry pie that Ms. Ida had sitting on the kitchen windowsill cooling off.

I rushed into the house and straight to the kitchen. "Hi, Ms. Ida," I said as my eyes gazed at the many pots on the stove. I didn't care to guess what was in each; I knew it was going to be something really good. I made my way to my room and put down my school supplies before heading back to the kitchen and out to the backyard to wash up.

"Are you ready to eat?" Ms. Ida asked as I rushed by.

"I sure am," I said as the door slammed behind me. I looked to the window from the yard. Ms. Ida was smiling as she hummed a song and began to put food on a plate for me.

That evening, as grandpa and I sat out on the porch, he asked me more about how my day at school had gone. I felt a bit more at ease after hearing that he understood how good it was for me to be with people my own age.

"It went good," I said with a smile on my face. "All of the new kids I met on the bus already knew something about me, and they all knew you."

"Well, that's good," he said. "I was hoping you had a good time, knowing that you must miss the schoolin' you gets up north."

"I did wonder what it was going to be like since I've realized that I'm not going back home," I said. I didn't really want to think about it since it made me sad to think about.

"Yo' mama talked to me and asked if I'd mind lookin' after you for a while, and since me and Ida ain't got nobody here but us, I wanted to have this time to really get to know you," he said. "I was hoping you wouldn't mind."

"Oh no," I said, "I really like it here, and now that I'm going to school, I think I'm gonna like it even more, when I get to know more friends."

"I sho hopes so," Grandpa said as he lit his cigarette. "I sho hopes so."

We sat there for some time looking at the stars. Somehow there seemed to be more of them than I had seen before. Grandpa talked a bit about his days on the railroad, and I daydreamed about what school was going to be like the next day, wondering if I'd get the same seat and get to sit next to Allyson again. Suddenly I heard my grandpa's voice: "It's time to get ready fo' bed. You have to get up early fo' school."

I leaped up out of my seat. I was more than ready to go to bed. The sooner I did, the sooner I'd wake and be on my way. I did get to bed, but sleep didn't come easy.

It seemed to take forever for me to walk the distance to the highway. I waited and waited, but the school bust just wasn't coming. After a while the cars with the flashing lights began to come from the other direction. They were in a hurry to get to where they were going. There, too, were ambulances and signed police cars—something was very wrong, and it in in the direction my school bus should have been coming from. After some time, the ambulances and police cars and other cars with the flashing lights began coming back toward me; they were moving at top speed. The last thing on the road was a tow truck, and it was towing my school bus.

The bus was mangled and twisted metal from the front to the back. I could see the seat where Allyson and I sat yesterday: it was crushed and bent out of shape. I wondered if she was sitting there and was now in one of the ambulances I saw heading back toward our school. I thought about all my schoolmates and how they were after whatever happened to the school bus. I began to cry as I walked down the highway, wanting only to get to where my new friends were. I needed to know how they were doing.

"Al, wake up. It's time for you to get up." I heard a familiar voice calling out to me. "Get up and get ready for school," grandpa said as he left the room.

It was a dream and a bad one at that. I sat up in the bed and looked around the room. It was just a dream, I said to myself and smiled as the rooster began its morning wake-up call. I could smell the bacon cooking in the kitchen and could hear Ms. Ida singing as she did often when cooking. I thought about the dream for a minute, thankful that it was just that a dream. I went about my morning ritual, then made my way down the road toward the highway. It wasn't long before the bus arrived. I climbed aboard and sat with Allyson.

Allyson and I talked all the way to the school. I quickly realized that I liked her a lot, but Southern girls were not so easy to get as girlfriends. At some point you had to meet and talk to their families before you could even ask them out. I remembered all of this from the time I was here before and my aunt Neat wanted to go out with a boy from school and she had to bring him to meet Grandpa.

We exited the bus and went on our way to class. According to my schedule, my first class was English. When I got there, most of the other students where already seated. I got to my desk and saw this book on it—it must have been the biggest book I had ever seen. I looked around and saw that every desk had the same book on it. Mrs. Bolton entered the room and asked the class to turn the book over to the side with the title on it. As I did so, I read to myself, *Great Expectations*. My mind was still on the question of just what we were supposed to do with the giant book, but my question was quickly answered when Mrs. Bolton told the class that we were to read the large book and turn in a book report on it. I turned to look at my other classmates. We were all probably thinking the very same thing: When?

It was not until the end of the class, after having also been assigned some other reports, that we learned that the report on the giant book was not due for some time. We were, however, instructed to read some of it daily because during the school term we might be quizzed on it and that could count toward our final grade. I was just happy that it wasn't something that had to be done right away. That book I for sure was gonna take quite some time to read, and if it were due quickly, that would mean reading every waking chance I had, including weekends, and I wanted to spend some time with Allyson even if it meant going through her kinfolk. I liked her that much.

I finally got to meet Allyson's grandparents. It appeared that she was in the same boat as me, living with them. I wondered why—if perhaps her parents just didn't want her around, as was the case with me—but she quickly said after the introduction that her mother and father were at another location where they are working and building a house. Allyson's grandmother was a heavy woman with pretty long gray hair; her grandfather was a light-skinned man, slender but well built. When I was introduced to him, he gave me a look that could have had several meanings, all of which I didn't want to think about. Her grandmother nodded and said hello to me; that was as nice as it was going to get.

We were at an after-school function, and her grandfather was not excited about being there. Allyson and I did get to talk to each other for a short time, and that was good enough for me. After the event, I looked for my ride home and saw Allyson leave with her grandparents. I had no idea if I was in or out with them; I just had to wait and see. It was going to be a long weekend for me.

That Saturday morning, I awoke to the sound of the old truck. That usually meant Grandpa was going to town or to the various markets. I hurried to the backyard to throw some water on my face. I wanted to go with him. I liked the way he handled himself with the white folks he encountered on these tripes, and he always had something to say to me that seemed useful, even if I didn't always quite understand the full meaning of his words. Ms. Ida saw me rushing and must have realized that I was not going to stay around for some breakfast, so she made me a sandwich and handed me a jug of sweet tea as I rushed toward the front door. To my surprise, Grandpa was standing at the truck with the side door open, signaling me to come and get in. He was waiting for me; Ms. Ida must have called to him to do so.

The ride to town was nice as always. Grandpa asked me about the night before, and I told him about meeting Allyson's grandparents. I should have known that in a town like this, nearly everybody knew everybody. He quickly said that he knew them and how nice they both were. I wondered if he really knew them 'cause from my first impression, she was nice, but he was not so nice.

That was the beginning of the first lesson of the day: Grandpa talked about the importance of family and how essential it was to protect the woman of the family. He reminded me that Allyson's grandparents had a right to see that she was all right and that meant where I was concerned. He went on to explain that what I needed to do was show myself as someone who also cared about Allyson and would protect her.

"A man's responsibility to woman is to care bout them in every manner," he went on to say. "Listen to what da say and respect them. Iffin you do dis, no woman's people would wish harm to ya."

Boy, did I have a lot to think about. grandpa's words just kept ringing in my ears, and of course I knew that he was right. I remembered the time when Mama and Daddy had words that seemed to go against each other. Daddy left the house, and when he returned, he had a bunch of flowers for Mama. She didn't want to take them at first, but after some more words from Daddy, she took the flowers, and the rest of the night when smoothly. I could only think that Daddy must have had this same talk with Grandpa.

We went to some of the same places we had gone to before and to three I had never been to. At one the white owner seemed almost nice until we were about to leave, and he said to my grandpa, "Boy, you be sho to come back by next week iffin ya can. It seems that the folks like yo' sweet corn and melons."

Grandpa looked at me as I got into the truck. He spat on the ground, climbed into the truck, and said, "Sho will. Sho will."

As we drove off, he said, "He sho won't be getting any dees melons nor corn from me next week." He looked at me, and we both laughed as we began the drive home.

As we drove up, I could smell the aroma of apple pie coming from around the house. Ms. Ida always left them in the window to cool. Sometimes, if we had made ice cream, we would cut into it while it was still warm. We unloaded the few items that were left on the truck. This had been a good outing for grandpa: I had seen him collecting money at every stop except where he dropped off some bags to a white family with children running around barefoot and looking unkept and when he dropped off a sack of stuff at the place where we stopped to use the outhouse.

I finished putting the empty crates away and rushed into the house. I wanted to know what else was going on in that kitchen. Ms. Ida pointed the way to the back door and motioned for me to go and wash up. When I got there, grandpa was already cleaning up; I'm sure that he, too, wanted to get to whatever Ms. Ida had cooked. He waved for me to hurry up. When I got to the table, the plates were set up, and we bowed our heads as Grandpa said grace.

"Good Lord, thanks ya fo' dis blessing' of food you provided to dis table, thanks ya fo' the day and all its blessings, and Lord, keep us in yo' care, lookin out fo' one another and carin' fo' others, we pray in Jesus's name. Amen."

I was the first to hand my plate over to Grandpa for a slice of the roast that was sitting in the middle of the table. I went on to take a slice of corn bread and a large scoop of the green beans with butter dripping down them. We sat quietly as we enjoyed the meal. Then came the apple pie. I could tase all the ingredients: the buttery crust, the nutmeg and cinnamon, a slight bit of salt, and sugar. This was good.

Sundays always began with a big breakfast, followed by some TV to hear the church groups sing before we went off to church. Grandpa liked to listen to them, and as I've said, on occasion we'd drive for miles after church to go to where the actual groups would sing live. Sometimes Grandpa would also go out of his way to attend country music concerts. I must admit that I kinda liked them too and would look forward to the times we would pack up food and water—that was a signal that we were not coming straight home and possibly would be out for the day.

There, too, was the Sunday dinner that was always a special treat. Ms. Ida would be up early to roast a whole chicken or a ham. And there was also the possibility that some family members would stop by to spend the day. I would get to meet cousins I didn't know or uncles and aunts I had never met; it was always fun seeing the interactions of my family members. Or it could be just us enjoying a good church service and going home to have a good meal and rest up to get ready for the upcoming week ahead.

This Sunday we came home. The church service was long, and the heat coming in from the open windows made it a bit uncomfortable. I was glad when the sermon ended, and I was able to go outside and get a drink of water from the well. The water was cold, and for a moment, I thought of what it would be like to pour some over my head just to cool off.

Grandpa signaled for me to come to the car. I guess he was ready to get out of the heat as well. Ms. Ida was already seated, and I climbed into the front next to her. The church was only a twenty-minute drive away, so it wasn't long before we were pulling into the driveway. I got out and reached to help Ms. Ida out. Grandpa parked the car and came into the house a few minutes after we did. Ms. Ida went straight for the kitchen. I went to my room and got out of my Sunday clothes before heading to the kitchen also. I could hear grandpa in the backyard; he was washing up. Ms. Ida looked at me and I knew that I needed to do the same, so I left the kitchen and went to where the washbasins were. Grandpa was done and going back into the house. I washed as quickly as possible and went back into the kitchen. Grandpa was in the living room, and I knew that I should probably go there too and leave Ms. Ida to getting dinner ready.

Dinner was a hit as usual. I was completely stuffed after and decided to catch up on some reading. After all, I still had that giant book to go through. There would be time later to sit on the porch with grandpa and hear about his time with the railroad or something that took place long ago that he wanted to share with me. Sometimes the stories would be funny.

I read for a while, then went to the front porch where grandpa was sitting. The huge swing was my favorite place to sit. It faced sideways, and I could see the entire porch from there. Grandpa asked me about my reading, and I explained that it was going to take me some time to finish that book since it was so much to read.

"Book learnin' is good fo' ya," he said. "Itta be the one thing can't nobody take from ya. When ya knows whatcha knows, you could stand on dat, an can't nobody move ya."

As I listened to his words, even with the difficulty in sometimes completely understanding, I could hear the logic; I could hear the reasoning. I knew that there was much I could learn from this man even though he couldn't read or write, and he signed his name with an X.

"I know you're right, Grandpa" I said, "and I'll certainly try to learn as much as I can from both my school and from you." grandpa smiled.

The next morning, as I waited for the school bus to arrive, I realized that I had a different view of Allyson and of her grandpa. I felt a sense of responsibility for her well-being. I wanted to look after her and keep her safe even from my teenage desires. I certainly didn't want to see any kind of harm come to her. I knew enough not to ever put my hands on her; I had learned that from my father. I remembered having pulled my sister's hair. What a mistake that turned out to be. Daddy heard Rosalind's scream and was on me before I knew it. My hair was in no way as long as my sister's, but Dad was able to piece enough for me to feel the pain of it. He went on to tell me that I should never ever put my hands on a girl or woman in a way that would hurt them in any way. That along with a week's house punishment taught me a valuable lesson.

The bus arrived, and I took my seat next to Allyson. I asked her how her weekend had gone and listened carefully as she described it. She talked all the way to school as I looked at her and realized that I really liked her a lot.

The day was going well until Gary, a boy who was in my math class, bumped me. It was hard, and I knew for sure he had wanted to do it. He had been looking at me for days with a look that my New York City experience knew was a challenge. For a split second, I just wanted to haul off and punch him in the face. Back home that's how you had to handle things sometimes, or the bullies who pick on you every day. They would even take things from you if you didn't fight back. The thought quickly passed when I remembered that rather than reacting to things, I should ask myself or someone else, "What is a better way to handle this?" I gave him a look that was meant to say "You really don't want to mess with me" but ended it with a smile. He said he was sorry and walked on. I knew that at some point he and I were going to clash.

That night after supper, as grandpa and I sat out on the porch in our usual positions, I thought it a good time to talk about what had happened in school with Gary. I wanted to hear what he thought about how I was feeling about it and to hear some of his wisdom on how I should handle the matter. I felt it best to just spit it out, so I did just that: "grandpa, this kid in one of my classes has been giving me some bad looks, and today he bumped into me pretty hard. I think he means me harm and that I may have to fight him at some point." I waited for what seemed a long minute before Grandpa answered.

"Fighting is not the answer," he said. "Iffin someone calls you out and makes it known that they's wantin' to hurt you, well dat's a different thing. Then you have a right to fight back. Sometimes folk just don't know how to get wit' other folk, so's dey acts out. Give it some time to see which one dis is."

I thought about what grandpa said, still anticipating that at some point this situation was gonna have a bad outcome, but it was worth it to not be the one who got things started: I could hold off and see just where this went and allow him to make the first move. Again, I realized that it was a good idea to talk with grandpa before going off on my own idea. His way did seem to make more sense than mine did.

The next day at school, when I saw Gary, I tried to figure out if the look he was giving me could mean something else. Suddenly, it didn't look so threatening; there was more of a curiosity than a threat. I wondered if this was what grandpa was talking about. Maybe all Gary wanted to do was get to know me better, and he just didn't know any other way to do that than to act combative. That would explain his behavior and would prove Grandpa right.

Midway through our math class, Mr. Bolton asked us to form groups of five to work on some equations. He wanted us to use math to highlight situations and find conclusions also using math. My first thought was to see if Gary wanted to be in an alliance with me, so I went over to him and asked. I could see right away that he was pleased and wanted to work in my group. He also suggested that we pick two other classmates, people I would not have normally asked, and his choices were good ones. I picked one more, and we began working on the problem. We made a great team and came up with a marketing problem and a solution that received a high mark. The problem, or at least what had I thought was the problem, with Gary was also solved.

CHAPTER 10

We had just completed our midterm exams. I was excited because there was the upcoming break from school and the prospect of the holidays. This was my first holiday away from home, and I had no idea just what it was going to be like, but it was still the holidays so it could not be so bad. I was sure that I wasn't going home to New York; I had received a letter from Mama wishing me a happy holiday season, and of course there was some money for me to buy something for myself. I did miss the decorations of the city, the Christmas trees and bright lights that were just about everywhere you went. Grandpa did not have that going on. We didn't have a Christmas tree, or bright lights, and things were a good bit different. There was a sense of joy in the air: people would come by just to sit and talk and have a cold drink.

One night we went to another farm where there was a whole pig on a wooden stick being turned from time to time by the owner to make sure that the flames would reach each part. Down the road there was a barn fire going on, and people just gathered around telling stories and singing songs. Yes, there was something different all right, and we were as much a part of it as anyone.

Grandpa's smokehouse was filled with meats that had been hanging in there for weeks, even months. Sometimes when people would come over, he'd go in the smokehouse and come out with a large ham wrapped in cloth and hand it to them, wishing them a happy holiday.

Then there was that day when several trucks pulled up to the house. I could feel that there was something different about this situation. There was always a rifle within hand's distance from the door, and as Grandpa went to see who was there, his hand went to grab it. He instructed me to stay where I was as he stood in the doorway. I could hear a voice from outside say, "Howdy, Mr. Golden" in a deep Southern drawl. Grandpa replied in the same manner, now with the rifle in his hand.

"We's wondering iffin we could hunt on a bit of yo' land," the voice said. "There's some deer running through, and we'd like to get a few iffin dat il be OK with you."

I watched as Grandpa put the rifle back into its position near the doorway. "Sho, go 'head," Grandpa said.

"We'll stop by when we's leaving," the voice said just before I heard the engine roaring. Then the trucks left the yard area.

Later that day the trucks returned, and they were loaded with deer that had been shot and now splayed across each other in the backs of the trucks. Grandpa went out and spoke with the men, who took one of the deer to the back of the house and into a shed as instructed by Grandpa. It was where Grandpa would take animals before they ended up in the smokehouse. I had never been in there and didn't ever want to.

The men got back into their trucks and drove off, and Grandpa returned from the shed. He went into the kitchen and talked to Ms. Ida. My only thought was that we were gonna be eating that deer at some point, and I wasn't sure if I wanted to do that. I had never had deer for dinner and could only think that it would not be as good as chicken or fish or ham, those meats that I'd been eating all my life. I did think back on the day we were at a neighbor's farm some months before and I ate turtle, which I must say was quite good, and the time Ms. Ida served us some possum stew; it was good also. Just maybe there is something to this country living and eating the wild animals that are here, I though. I'll make a judgment on the deer when it comes time to do so.

The holiday season was about to end when I awoke with a terrible stomach pain. I could hear Grandpa in the outer room, so I called out to him. When he came into my room, I told him of my pain. He asked if I needed to go to the bathroom. I did, but that was not the cause of my pain, I tried to explain. He suggested that I go there first before anything else, so I did. I could hardly walk the pain was so great. I moved slowly and was bent over. I sat in the outhouse for about twenty minutes, but there was no relief from the pain. When I got back to the house, I was met by Grandpa with a cup of hot tea. He asked if I had gone to the bathroom. I had, but the pain was still there. He instructed me to drink the tea and lie back down.

This was getting serious. I had had this pain for three days, and it only seemed to get worst. Grandpa was by my side most of the time, and Ms. Ida brought me my meals, some of which I just couldn't eat due to the pain I was in. I could hear grandpa's car as it drove off down the road. He had not done driven off in the days that I was sick, so I wondered what he was doing leaving me at a time like this. I had grown accustomed to him staying with me or really close by whenever I was not feeling well.

Grandpa was gone for some time before I heard the car returning. He came into my room and announced that I would be going to the hospital. He helped me to put some clothes on, and Ms. Ida washed my face from a pail of water she had brought into the room. Grandpa lifted me out of the bed and carried me to the car. As Ms. Ida opened the door, he put me in the front passenger side seat. I had been in this position many times before while driving with Grandpa going here or there and usually would be happy to be there, but this was different. I was not feeling well and was going to the hospital; I had never been to a hospital before and wasn't sure if this was good.

Grandpa drove for more than an hour, sometimes faster than I had ever seen him drive before. Then were pulled up to a large building. It reminded me of the buildings in New York since it had many floors. Grandpa rushed out and into the building, shortly coming out with a chair with wheels on it. He lifted me into the chair and pushed me through the large glass doors to where men in white coats were waiting. I was put on a bed, and the men started touching my stomach area. The pain became greater and greater. I heard them say I needed to be rushed into surgery. By then some of my pain was starting to go away as I drifted into sleep.

As I opened my eyes, I could tell that I was in a room where machines with different sounds were going off. I attempted to move but was too weak to do so. I tried to remember what had happened to me. I remembered Grandpa bringing me through the large glass doors and the men with the white coats touching me where the pain was. After that I didn't remember very much. I looked around the room with the neck movement I could muster and realized that I was alone even though I could hear voices in the background. I even thought that I heard Mama's voice, so I assumed that I must still be dreaming.

The voices became clearer and clearer. One still sounded like Mama. I looked over to where the voices were coming from and saw that it really was Mama; she was coming into the room and heading toward me. I wanted to reach up to hug her, but I just couldn't get up enough strength to do so. She came over to me and asked how I was feeling. I could see the concern in her face, but there was also something that I had not seem in a long time in her. It was a sense of peace. She did not have that worried look that I so often saw when she had to deal with something I had done.

I spent more than a week in the hospital. I had to learn how to walk again due to the surgery. I had a long scar on my stomach area, so when I walked, I was bent over. Mama would come to see me every day, and I found out that I had family in the town where the hospital was located. When I was finally able to leave the hospital, still walking bent over but not as much as before, we went to see my uncle (Mama's brother) and his family. That was also when I met my cousin George "Butch" Atkinson. He was a bit older than I was, but we got along quite well.

I didn't realize it, but I was soon to be headed back to my grandpa's house and Mama would be going back to New York. As the visit to my uncle's was going on, Grandpa was on his way to pick me up. When the doorbell rang and I saw Grandpa standing there, I knew it was over—my time with Mama was ending. I wanted to cry but held back the tears. I was not gonna let her know that I wanted to spend more time with her. I wanted her to see that I was a big boy and could understand my fate, so I said my goodbyes, gave Mama a big hug, and headed to the waiting car.

Mama and Grandpa talked for a while, both seeming to agree with what was being said by nodding their heads. After a time, grandpa came to the car, and I looked out the passenger side to see Mama, Butch, and Uncle George waving goodbye. As we drove off, I still couldn't let myself cry, although I wanted to so badly.

There was silence for a while, then Grandpa asked me how I was. I wanted to tell him that I wanted to spend more time with Mama, but he spoke before I could think it through.

"Yo' mama loves you," he said, "and I know it 'because she told me how much she misses you. When I told her that you were so sick dat I couldn't do nuffin fo' you, she was upset with me and told me to take you to the hospital. Dat's love.

"Sometimes you just don't see da love; you just gotta know in ya heart dat it's there 'cause of what peoples do, and yo' mama came down here to help look after you outta dat love she has fo' ya. A family love doesn't always sho up in ways ya see clearly, but it does sho up in what da do fo' ya."

I had never thought about looking at what Mama did for me before that moment. Mama and I had spent a lot of time together, I began to remember. She would also read my writings as I brought them to her for her approval; she'd read them out loud and compliment me on my newfound skill even though she would sometimes have to help me with my spelling. I guess it was her way of saying she loved me.

Yet she still sent me away. What was that about? I thought to myself. Then I remembered how Mama looked the first time I saw her in the hospital. She had that look I had not seen before; she was not worried or sad as I had seen her in the past—there was a peace about her. Maybe I was the problem, not Mama. Maybe it's me, I thought. Maybe I am the one that has to change, not Mama.

The rest of the ride was quiet; I had a lot to think about. I looked at the road ahead and thought about what I needed to do different. I had to change some things so that I didn't cause Mama to ever get that old look back. I liked the way she looked now. I might need to talk to Grandpa about this at some time, and maybe he'd be able to help me get back home to New York someday.

The drive took about an hour and a half, and as we drew nearer, I began to get excited. I had been eating hospital food for some time and was wondering just what might be waiting for us when we got home. I was sure that Ms. Ida had made something special as she would on occasions when she wanted to surprise me.

As we approached the house, I could see Ms. Ida standing in the doorway, I could see that big smile she always had. I realized that I had missed her a lot. I was still not walking standing straight up, but I made my way out the car and rushed over to greet her.

"Hi, grandma," I said, not realizing that that was the first time I had called her that. I gave her a big hug and looked up to see that she was crying. I wondered why she was crying, but she quickly wiped her eyes and walked me to the kitchen. There was a cherry pie on the window, and the stove was filled with pots of food.

"Go wash up," she instructed. "I'll make you something to eat." She wiped her eyes again.

"I sure will," I said, still wondering what was in those pots but knowing that I would have to leave some room for the cherry pie.

Grandpa was coming into the kitchen after taking the small bag of things I had from the hospital to my room. He met me in the backyard, where I was washing up for dinner.

"It sure smells good in the kitchen," I said to him as I toweled the water from my face.

"She been at it all day," he replied. "She wanted it to be special fo' ya."

It was a great meal: peas and rice, baked macaroni, and fried chicken. This was all the things I really liked in one meal, and I managed to save room for a slice of cherry pie.

After dinner I finally made my way into my room. My bed was full of papers. My teacher had given Grandpa all of my homework assignments so that I could catch up. There was also an envelope with red and blue trim; I had seen this type of envelope before, when my father would send us a personal letter for the holidays. Each one of us would get a letter from him as he was not home for most holidays; the letter would be his way of keeping in touch with us and letting us know that he hadn't forgotten.

I looked over the homework first. It didn't look to difficult; I would have to do some reading, but that wasn't a problem. I looked at the envelope and decided that I'd open it after I finished my reading assignments and homework. Dad's letters were usually intense, and I wanted to have nothing else on my mind when I got into it.

It took me a little over two hours to finish my homework. I could hear Ms. Ida in the kitchen; she always sang while she cooked. I couldn't imagine what else she'd cook after all the food that she had prepared earlier, but she was cooking something, that was for sure. I went in to sit with her, having not done so in a while. I think I was also curious about just what she was cooking. She and I always had good talks when we got the chance to do so, like when Grandpa was in the field or if he was out visiting with his friends on a weeknight or a Saturday evening.

As I entered the kitchen, I saw that whatever it was, it was in the oven. I just came out and asked, "Grandma, what are you baking?"

As she turned toward me, I could see her big smile. "You remember when I made that sugar cake fo' you and you said you liked it?" she answered. "I thought I'd make you one now."

I did remember I did really like it. I asked her if it was hard to make back then, and she said it took a bit of time, which was why she didn't make it much. Wow, I thought, that cake that's hard to make she's making for me. "Thank you," I said as I walked over to give her a hug.

I sat down, and we talked for a while. When the cake came out of the oven, she asked if I wanted a piece while it was hot. I remembered trying that the first time: it was a bit too much for me to handle, and I burned my tongue. "No, I'll wait until it cools," I said, really wanting to take the chance as it looked so good but not wanting to burn myself again. I went back to my room.

I didn't know where grandpa had gone. I did hear the car start up, so he must have gone to visit someone. As this community was, he may have gone around to let people know that I was back home. After all, tomorrow being Sunday, I'd see most of them in church.

I had time before the cake cooled, so I decided to read the letter from my father. I gently opened the envelope and removed the two pages. Dad had good handwriting; the letters where large and distinct, each word clear and concise. My brother Jobbie had pretty much the same handwriting. Mine was small but readable. I looked at the return address, and I saw that he was mailing it from Hong Kong. I didn't have a map nearby but knew that it was a very long way from where I was. It had also been sent to my address in New York, so I wondered if he knew that I had been sent away by Mama. I wondered how upset he would be not seeing me when he came home. He and I would spend so much time together when he was in the kitchen cooking. He'd tell me stories about the many places he had gone to while working on the ship.

I sat up in the chair in my room and began to read the letter:

My Dear Son Al,

As I sit down to write this, I can only wonder how you are doing, especially since you are not home with the rest of the family. I know you must be feeling out of sorts and maybe even left out or alone. I want you to know that the decision to send you away was not an easy one for your mother or for me.

We simply wanted to keep you safe from the things that are going on in New York. We thought about it for a while and felt that the risk of something happening to you was just too great for us to just allow you to stay with the chance of you getting hurt in any way. We did it out of our love for you and the need for us as parents to look out for you.

We also thought carefully about where to send you. We knew that my father would be a good caregiver and provider for you. As he was for me as a child. We knew that you'd be in good hands with him and that he would look after you with all that care that a parent would be expected to give to a child, so I hope that you will understand what may have been bothering you and see that you are as important to us as any of your brothers or sisters.

Now, I hope that your Christmas and New Year went well. You are having an experience that even I haven't had. I did visit the farm you're staying on, but you get to see the whole workings of it.

I hope you have friends and are doing things that you never would have been able to do in New York. I like that you are seeing and doing things that we could only think about and maybe someday do. As I said, I have been there, and I'm sure that you must be riding horses and milking cows and planting things and watching them grow. Those are things that most people never in a lifetime get to do.

I can't wait for us to get together and share stories. I walked around some very old churches today and saw people dressed in long gowns lighting candles until the whole place lit up so bright I could see large statues. It was a sight to behold.

> I'm sure that you have some new stories to tell me, and some are yet to come. How's school? I hope it wasn't a really hard adjustment from city to country living. Things must be so different, and I gotta ask, do you have a girlfriend?
>
> Well, I hope I cleared up some stuff for you. I certainly miss you and wish you the very best holiday season. Take good care of yourself and do your best to get through this most trying time and be sure that we are in it too. Love you so much, Dad.

I folded the letter and put it back into the envelope. Yes, you did clear up some stuff for me, Dad, I thought. Now I knew that he, too, was in on me being here away from home, but the problem wasn't me as I had thought. It was good to hear the part about sharing with each other, that told me that I might be going back home someday. There was the hope I needed to get by.

As I sat there for a moment, I heard grandpa's car return. I thought back to what Dad had said in the letter, and I remembered how when I was sick before, he would be there by my side when I awoke. I remembered the cool towels he would place on my head the medicine he would give me and the time he fed me food when I was too weak to feed myself. I thought back to Dad's words: "We knew that you'd be in good hands with him and that he'd look after you with all the care a parent would be expected to give a child." I realized that there was love all around me and that all I had to do was figure out how to conduct myself in a way that would not cause Mama to have to worry about me when I did get to go back home, whenever that was.

I got up and went out to meet grandpa as he walked up the steps to the house. I saw a different man that day, and my heart was heavy. I hugged him, and although he didn't know why, he hugged me back. I felt a strength in him that I wanted for myself. He, like my father, became my mentor.

Grandpa and I went in the house and straight to the kitchen, where Ms. Ida was sitting at the table. The cake was there waiting to be cut. I looked at grandpa, and he looked back at me. We knew there was only one thing left to do, so we headed for the washbasins and rushed back to our seats at the table. Grandma Ida cut us a large slice of cake for each of us, and we three ate in silence. There was no need for words.

CHAPTER 11

Sunday's church service was amazing. I felt very special since the entire church sang and prayed for me. I truly felt much better after that and was looking forward to getting back to school the next day.

It was hard for me to sleep that night. I went to bed early hoping that I'd sleep through the night and awake ready to see all my friends. Even though some had come by the house to see how I was doing, there were others I hadn't seen in what seemed like forever.

The rooster was especially loud as he sounded the alarm that morning was here. I jumped up. As I had already set my clothes out before I went to bed, there was no need to look for an outfit to wear. I could hear grandma Ida in the kitchen doing what she did so well, preparing a breakfast for grandpa and me. I rushed to the back door so that I could wash up and get ready for school.

"Good morning," I said as I rushed out the back door.

Grandma Ida turned, holding a kettle of hot water, which I needed to use for my washup. As I touched the pail's contents, I could feel that it was just too cold for me to use, so I turned and headed back toward the back door; I realized that I should have taken the kettle.

"Thank you," I said as I reached for the kettle. I poured it into the pail, which made the water so that I could use it for my washup. When I was done, I rushed back to my room to put on the clothes I had selected for my return to school. I looked in the mirror and smiled at my reflection; I had come a long way since my appendix operation and having to learn how to stand up straight. I was ready to get back into circulation, maybe even hang out with the guys after school and horseback-ride again, all of which I hadn't done since my illness.

More than anything I wanted to see Allyson, so I quickly ate breakfast and started making my way to the bus stop. Grandpa looked at me and smiled as I headed out the door. Even he knew that I was leaving a bit early.

As I waited for the bus for what seemed forever, I was going over what I was gonna say to her. I thought, Should I talk about my experience, or should I ask her about what she has gone through since I last saw her? Should I start with asking about her grandparents? Maybe I'll just wait for her to talk first and go from there.

I looked down the highway again and saw the bus coming. There was no more time to think; this was it, I thought to myself as the bus stopped and the doors opened for me to enter. I stepped on, and the entire bus shouted, "Welcome back, James!" I hadn't expected that, and it made me tear up. I quickly wiped my eyes and began walking toward my seat, which was next to Allyson, thanking everyone I passed along the way.

When I reached my seat, Erick was sitting there; he motioned me to keep moving to the back of the bus. I looked at Allyson to see if there was some sign of her being in line with this new arrangement, and she didn't even look at me. Suddenly, this was turning into the saddest day of my life. As I continued past the seat with my newfound sadness, everybody started to laugh. Erick got up and motioned me back to my seat next to Allyson. She was laughing also. It was a prank, and the joke was on me. After a long second, I too started to laugh.

After I sat down, Allyson began the conversation by saying she had missed me very much and was happy to see me back. She went on to say that she was being told about my progress by the friends that had come by the house to check in on me. I had wondered if she knew how I was doing and was glad she was aware of my progress.

School was great, and it was so good to see all of the friends I missed. Grant ran over from his bus as soon as he saw me getting off mine. It was good to see him also. He filled me in on an upcoming project in the class we shared. I quickly said that he could count me in.

The rest of the school day went well. It was great to hand in all the homework for my classes and to know that I was not lagging behind in any of my subjects. The ride home was also good since there was no one sitting in my seat next to Allyson. She and I talked the whole ride to my stop. As I walked the roadway to grandpa's, my thoughts were back on the bus: it was so good to see all my friends and especially to see and talk to Allyson. She was still my girl, and that mattered a lot to me.

The week went by quickly. I had made plans to hang out with some of the guys after school. Punch would give me a ride home after the activities at school, and I would get to spend more time with Allyson. At the school I saw my science teacher, who was surrounded by my classmates. I wandered over to see what that was all about. It appeared that there was an opportunity to go on a field trip with him to a local college, and just for going there, points would be added to your grade. I liked the sound of that. He said that there would be more information forthcoming. He left it at that and went to his car. I could see that all who had heard about the trip were also interested in going, and so was I—not so much because of the extra points but because I really liked science and thought that there would be something in going for me.

The rest of the night I spent walking and talking with Allyson until her grandparents came to pick her up. I realized I liked the after-school events here; that had not been the case back in New York.

The weeks went by, and we were coming to our midterm break. I always looked at that time to see where I was at with my grades and plans for the end of the school year. I was doing pretty well with my grades and had found out that I was not a very good athlete: I tried out for the football team and saw the hits that were given and decided that I wouldn't want to go through that. I was a bit too short to try basketball since the guys on the team were all a good bit taller than I, and I just wasn't good at getting the ball to go into the hoop. I did like track and field and found a place in that arena. More than anything I liked reading and writing and acting.

I still enjoyed the time spent with grandpa on the weekends and the times I would listen to him tell me stories about his life. I gathered that he must have really liked the time he spent working on the railroad trains. He spoke about that often, and he was a good storyteller as well as teacher. I learned so much about being a man and the responsibility that goes along with that. I also realized that even as a young man, I had to step up and do some things to help my household. I had never really given that much thought in the past, and now that I was learning these things, I realized that even my behavior in school and the friends I was around could have a good or bad influence on my life and on my family.

I realized that my coming to this place and spending time with this man was a gift and if I was just to use what I'd learned and continue to call on it throughout my life, I'd be better for it. I thought about Mama and all I had put her through: her having to come to school to be told that I was acting up in class, or the times that I was told not to go somewhere by her only to go anyway. And I remembered how I felt I needed to be a member of a gang even when Mama told me not to. Yes, I needed this place and this man and these friends to show me what was best for me. I also felt the need to tell Mama I was sorry for the things I had done and tell her that I understood why she wanted to send me away—it was not because she didn't like me; it was more that she loved me and didn't want the trouble I was heading for to overtake me.

As I thought about these things, I looked over at grandpa, who was sitting in the chair that was his reading place at the end of a day of framing. He was looking out at the fields he had plowed and planted seed on. I tried for a moment to figure out just what he thought as he looked around. I'd seen him sweat in the heat of the day in those fields. I'd eaten the corn, the beans, the watermelon.

I wondered if he was as proud of his labor as I was of him. I saw the man that had put all things aside to take care of me when I was sick and the man that told me to select the branch that I was to get a wiping with when I missed the school bus because I stayed out later than he instructed me to; it took me three tries to get the right one, and I knew that what I did was wrong, so I took what was coming to me and never did that again.

We sat for a good while just enjoying the night sky. grandma Ida came out and sat with us when she realized that we were not talking very much. I was glad that she did; she and I did get to spend time together when Grandpa would go out to visit friends, usually taking someone something from the farm. She chewed tobacco and would carry a can around when she did. I remember one day thinking that it would be a good idea for me to try some for myself. I snuck a little piece and began to chew. I was not sure of what to do next, so I swallowed some of the juice from it. That proved to be the one thing I shouldn't have done I had a problem for many days after that.

Grandma Ida was also a big part of my development while there. How could I have survived without the hearty meals she provided, not to mention her looking after my clothes and of course those times she and I would talk? I found her advice to be very helpful, and her smile, well, it just warmed me over.

Yes, Grandma Ida was special, though I wondered about her life since I never saw any of her family come by the house to see her. On the other hand, my family would show up on the weekends and Grandma Ida would spend hours in the kitchen cooking and baking for them. Even though when they showed up, they treated her very well, even embracing her as they would any family member, I could only imagine what she would have been like if her family had come to spend time with her.

We sat out for a bit longer before I felt I had to go in. I wanted to write a letter; I needed to tell Mama about the new me. I wanted to let her know that I understood how I must have been such a burden on her. I wanted her to know that I know how much it must have worried her when I was around. I needed to tell her that I had learned my lesson and was better for having spent this time away from her, where I could find this out about myself.

As I took out my pen and paper and looked down at the blank page, I wondered if I was on the right track with the way I was thinking about this letter. Maybe it should be more about my just missing her than me thinking in some way I knew what she was going through raising me, I thought. I've lived the sacrifice a family makes.

I've seen the love even through the pain families endure. I've heard the words of wisdom passed down from one family member to another. I needed to talk about this, and the wisdom I needed was sitting on the porch. I went back outside and asked them for help.

I think I made the right choice going back and asking for some guidance from grandpa and Grandma Ida. They suggested that I eliminate some of my thoughts and just talk about how I was doing and ask how she was doing, I could hear grandpa's words: "It's in da doing dat people see what you changed." And grandma Ida's: "Da love of a mama ain't to be understood by the churin all the time, and it don't need to be the churin trying to tell them about what it was like raising them."

That was the kind of advice I had become reliant on getting whenever I chose to ask for it, and I felt lucky to have these two to count on and a newfound understanding that it was OK to ask a grown-up for their help when I felt I needed it.

The weekend before I went back to regular classes, I was in my room when I saw grandpa carrying a basket full of fresh-picked corn onto the pickup truck. It had been a while since I went out with him because I would spend a lot of my time going places with my friends instead. I rushed out of the room and ran out to where he was picking up other cases of fruit and nuts. I saw the line of items that needed to be loaded and began to place them on the truck. As I looked over at grandpa, I could see the smile on his face even though he didn't say a word. We finished packing the truck, and Grandma Ida came over with a cloth sack in her hand.

"I packed y'all some lunch," she said as she handed me the sack. "Y'all take care."

I got into the truck as grandpa started it up. We hadn't said a word to each other until we were well on the way down the highway, and I asked, "Where we are heading, Grandpa?"

"We'z going to market in Elton. I promised that I'd bring them some fresh corn and nuts," he said, "so'z I's gonna keep my word, cuz ya knows word is bond."

When I awoke the next day, I reflected on that trip. I believe I got a little wiser each time I rode or spent time with grandpa; he always seemed to say something that I could agree with or see the value of in my own life. I think that's what I missed the most about my father. Sometimes his words were just lessons on what is right: "When you know right, you'll know wrong and which one to choose," I remember him telling me.

As I made my way down the road, I thought about these men that were such an influence on my life. I wondered where they got it from, this knowledge, this wisdom. I wondered if I'd be able to teach the same things someday. The break was nice, but it was good to get back into the routine that was school life, not to mention the fact it was good to see Allyson and the rest of my friends.

My grades were good. I had scored high in all ny subjects, and I couldn't wait to tell Grandpa about it. As I made my way home from the school bus, I was surprised when I didn't see Grandpa in any of the fields leading to the house; he would always be there, and I would get to talk to him before I got home. This time I really wanted to talk to him and tell him about my good grades, but he was nowhere to be found. I wondered if he was feeling well or if something had happened to him that made him have to stop work on the farm that day. My head was spinning. I began to pick up my pace—I wanted to see him.

As I made my way up the stairs toward the screen door, I could hear a familiar voice in the living room. It was my homeroom teacher Mrs. Bolton. I was reluctant to open the door. I wondered if there was something I had done wrong that she was here to tell Grandpa about. I stepped into the room expecting Grandpa's words to be harsh as he called out to me, but it was Mrs. Bolton that spoke first.

"Your grandfather and I were talking about you and your future," she said. "I was getting his permission to send you on a trip to look at the college opportunities available to you. I believe it's better to look into this before you have to make that decision, and this is as good a time as any for you to start."

I didn't know what to say, so I just looked at grandpa to get an idea as to what he was thinking about all of this. He, for the most part, just looked pleased that this whole conversation was taking place.

"Your grandfather has given his permission, so what do you think?" she asked.

I still hadn't taken my eyes off grandpa. He now had a small smile on his face. "I think if you say so, it probably is something that I should want to do, even if I still have another year before I'd have to make that decision."

"That's the point," she said. "I like students to have more information, so the sooner you start to look at the possibilities, the better choices you'll have when the time comes. It is much wiser that way, I assure you."

I finally felt that I could speak on my behalf and also felt that Grandpa was in agreement. "Yes, I'd love to do it," I said, still looking at grandpa. He smiled and nodded his head in agreement. Mrs. Bolton got up from her seat, went over to grandpa, and thanked him for allowing her the time to speak with him. She looked at me and said she'd see me tomorrow at school, at which time she'd give me more details.

Grandpa got up and walked her to the door and out into the shed where her car was parked. I realized that had I looked in there, I would have known that she was there and probably would have panicked trying to figure out what she was ding there. As she drove off and grandpa came back into the house again, I saw his smile, I felt his pride.

Weeks had gone by before the first visit to one of the colleges. There were only a few of us on the bus, and most of the others were already in their last year of high school. I counted five like myself that had another year of high school before going to college. grandma Ida had packed me a big lunch—the fried chicken was making me and others hungry. I knew it was a lot just by the weight of the bag it was packed in. A couple of the older guys had already begun to favor me and I knew that I was going to have to share some of it with them.

The drive took over two hours, and when we arrived, we were led straight to the cafeteria. It was time for me to see just what was in the sack grandma Ida had prepared. She must have somehow known that I would have a crowd around since she had packed four large pieces of chicken, as many biscuits, and a slice of peach pie, which I was not gonna share with anyone.

After lunch we were taken around the campus and shown all the sporting areas, the large gym, and the football field. Later we were shown the classrooms and the dormitories. At the end of the day, we were given pamphlets showing all the major attractions of the college and the courses it provided. I was impressed. Even though I hadn't given a lot of thought to what I wanted to study after high school, there did seem to be some good choices there.

Over the next three weeks, we visited three other colleges, each one highlighting something that was slightly different than what the others offered. All had a strong emphasis on higher learning. I knew that at some point I'd better figure out just what I was good at and what I wanted to be even better at. I loved writing, and I liked my English class and the subjects that came up in those courses; I just wasn't sure where to go with that.

The school season was winding down. It was the middle of May, and we were about to have our final exams. I felt pretty confident that I was doing to pass all of my subjects. It was also time to hand in my book report on *Great Expectations*. I really liked it a lot. I had finished reading it back in February and had put together a long list of notes on what I thought about it—the people, the situations, the storyline, and the ending. When I put it all together, it totaled twelve pages that I had to work from for my report. After going over all I had done in preparation, I was able to narrow it down to a five-page book report. I had discussions with some of my classmates and found that most had done a one- or two-pager. I wondered if what I had done was overkill, but after considering all I had put into my report, I thought it was appropriate to have detailed the assignment in the way I had. It was too late to change it now, and if I had done too much, the lesson I'd learn would probably help me in the future.

The finals took place throughout the week: I had two on Tuesday, one Wednesday, and two Thursday. My other classes had no finals, but the scores would still be announced on May 25, along with the other scores. On the days I had no finals, I could go to school and look over the schedules for the next year or hang out with other classmates who had finals or not go in at all. The school bus was running every day, as it did all season long. I chose to go in on Monday since Allyson had finals that day and we were to have lunch together.

I stayed home on Friday and planned to help grandpa around the farm. The new crops were coming up fast since there had been a good bit of rain over the past month after he did most of the planting. It was always nice to see the crops bursting out of the ground with their tiny leaves gleaming in the morning sun. It was a special time for me.

Grandpa and I cleaned up the stable and the corn shed where he kept the corn for the animals. It took us the better part of the morning to get that done. I was glad when Grandma Ida called us in for some lunch. As usual she went all out, and we had beet stew with baked bread buttered to perfection. After the meal we tackled the barn and the henhouse; that was a messy job, and I wished I had instead gone to school that day. But when it was all over, I could see the value I brought to the tasks of the day and was glad I had chosen to work side-by-side with grandpa. It would have been so much harder for him to do it all by himself.

Saturday, I slept in, ignoring the sound of the rooster that would sound off right outside my window each morning. I could hear grandma Ida in the kitchen and smell the bacon, but after yesterday all I wanted to do was sleep. I got another two hours of sleep before I felt I had better get up in case I was needed to do something else around the farm.

I got up and looked out the window. I had no idea what time it was, and I didn't really care about that. I could only hope that there wasn't a lot to do that day. I put on my pants and slipped my feet into my shoes. I could still hear Grandma Ida as I opened the door to my room. As I made my way to the back door, I saw her snapping beans.

"Good morning, grandma," I said. She looked up at me and nodded. I could see that big smile on her face.

I went outside and washed up in the pail of water that had been sitting in the sun for hours; it felt good on my face. I wanted to take a bath later on but thought that I had better see if there was something that I needed to do for grandpa before filling the large tub with water and setting it out to heat.

When I stepped back into the house, Grandma Ida had already set a plate of food on the table for me. I didn't realize just how hungry I was until I began to rush down the food. The grits were piping hot, as was the rest of the meal. I just don't know how she did it, but that was always the case in the morning even when I got up later that usual.

I wondered where grandpa was since I didn't see him when I went outside after breakfast. The truck was parked where he would have it when he was loading up for the market. I wondered if he was going today and if so, whether I could go with him. I always liked the time we spent together so I waited on the porch until he came into view. He had been in the watermelon field, which was down the road.

"Good morning," grandpa," I shouted out. He looked up and nodded back to me in a gesture of the same. "Are you going to market today?" I asked, pretty much knowing the answer to my question. I waited for his reply which came a bit slower that usual.

"I'll be going in a little while," he answered. "Does you want to go with me?"

"I sure do," I quickly replied.

"Iffin you want, you can pack some of the strawberries you planted," he said.

I looked over to the small patch of land he had given me to plant those strawberries. I was so proud of how they had come out and of the work I had put into tending them. The result was some of the biggest and sweetest strawberries I had ever seen. "I sure will," I said as I headed to the storage barn to get some small containers to place them in.

"When you is finished, put them in the back of the truck off to the side; we still have to put the melons in the truck," he said.

I nodded in agreement and rushed to pick the strawberries.

The ride was usually our time to talk. I would be excited to hear the words of wisdom that came through on these occasions, but for some reason grandpa was not as talkative as he should have been by then. I looked him over from the corner of my eye, trying not to be obvious; I wondered if there was something wrong but dared not ask lest I act out of place. We made our first stop and unloaded some of the watermelons and some of my strawberries. I was happy at the thought of the sale.

As we continued on to our next market, I mentioned how good I felt about the sale; I just had to break the ice and get some conversation going. Grandpa looked over at me and smiled.

"Dat's 'cuz you took good care to get good berries dat you is able to sell them," he said. "You is a bit of a farmer now."

I smiled as he said that. I realized that in all the time that I had been there and amid all the things I had tried to do to help around the farm, the little things, he had finally put me in the same category as himself. Yes, I was, like him, a farmer. I liked that.

When we got to the last stop, there was almost nothing left in the truck. My strawberries were gone after the fourth stop. I wasn't sure just how much money they had made or how much of it I was going to get to keep, and that didn't really matter. I had spent time and labor to work that little patch of land, and it had paid off. That's what mattered and nothing else.

We stopped at the small store outside of town, and grandpa removed a crate he had covered and took it inside. I wondered what it was that was covered in the back of the trunk. I see now that it was covered so that none of the other markets would see it and possibly want to buy it. It was there just for this market. This was where we stopped and were able to use the outhouse and the and the water to clean up.

I used the outhouse and washed my face and hands, then returned to the truck. It seemed a bit longer before grandpa came out and used the outhouse and washed up; he hadn't ever taken that long before. I was wondering if there was something wrong with him, just as I had thought when we were on the ride to our first stop. He just didn't seem to be his usual self—I hoped he was not sick or something. I didn't know how to ask that question. I could only hope that he'd say something that would open the door for me to ask.

As he got back into the truck, I could tell he had been drinking alcohol; I could smell it. I knew the smell because he would on occasion have a drink in the house, but it was aways in the evening and never in the day. There was something different about him, though he did seem better, as far as I could see, than when we started out earlier.

After a while he asked me what I thought I made on my strawberries. I wasn't sure of just what strawberries went for on the market, but I quickly said eight dollars. Grandpa looked at me, then smiled. "You made ten dollars," he said.

I didn't know what to say. I didn't really think I made eight dollars when I said it; I had just blurted out a number. I was happy at the thought I had earned my first money as a farmer and there was going to be much more in the future.

"If I can, I'd like to try something else for the next season," I said in my still-excited voice. "Maybe some other fruit or a vegetable. What do you think, grandpa?"

It was then that I saw that look I had seen earlier come back to his face. It took him a long time to answer. I was sure that he would agree with me. I was already listening for him to suggest blueberries or blackberries—I don't know, but I was sure that he would know something I could plant. Instead, just said, "Sure."

The weekend went well, even though I felt that grandpa was acting a bit different than he usually did when we went to town. Our talks were brief, and that was a big difference with times gone past. I was pretty sure that there was something going on with him and there was no way I'd ever get to know just what that was. Or maybe not. I could ask Grandma Ida, I thought. She may know.

Monday there was nothing much going on at school, so I stayed home. I did, however, get up early since I saw grandpa heading toward the stable from my room window. This may be a good time to ask Grandma Ida if grandpa is OK or if there is something going on with him that I should know about, I thought. I got up and rushed out of my room toward the kitchen.

"Good morning, Grandma Ida," I shouted as I passed by, wanting to hurry and wash up so I could get back to the kitchen and speak to her. She was my only hope of getting an answer to what was wrong with Grandpa.

I entered the kitchen. There was a plate of food set at my place at the table. I sat down and began my inquiry. "Grandma, is there something wrong with grandpa?" I asked. "He doesn't seem to be himself with me lately. Did I do something wrong? I waited for the long time it took for Grandma Ida to reply.

"Yo grandpa got a letter the other day, and whatsinever was in that letter has made him sad, and he ain't been the same since," she said. "I ain't fo'sure what was in that letter, but it got him down."

I sat there and thought about that for a minute. I was not aware of any letter. There were times when he'd ask me to read a letter that came for him, but this was not one of those times. I need to know more about that letter and where it came from, I thought.

Tuesday morning, as I waited by the bus stop, the letter was still on my mind. I just couldn't understand who could have written a letter that had such an impact on how grandpa would react toward me. He and I were getting along so well, what could come between us? As the bus approached, it came to me: I must have failed terribly in one or more of my classes. Yes, that would do it. One of my teachers must have come by the house and told him how poorly I had done in my class, or classes and he was upset with me. Maybe I could fix it by going to summer school and making up for any class I really messed up on. That would fix everything with me and Grandpa: I'd go to summer school, work hard, and correct the bad grades I got. After that grandpa and I would be all right again. I was excited because I now had the answer to the problem, and I knew just how to fix it.

The bus stopped, and I hopped on. I quickly saw Allyson and made my way to the seat beside her. I was glad to see her and everyone else on the bus that day.

"You look pretty happy," she said.

"I am," I answered. "I get to see you and everyone else, but of course especially you—that's a lot to be happy about."

"Yeah, I bet you say that to all your girlfriends," she said, laughing.

"Now, you know you're my only girl," I said, "and the only one I'd say that to."

The rest of the ride to school was just small talk and discussion about grades. I wasn't sure there was anything for me to be excited about as far as my grades were concerned, so I spoke just a little on the subject. My best bet was to wait and see just how much summer school I was gonna need. When the bus arrived at the school, I, like the rest of the students, rushed to where the grades were posted. I had all As and a B+.

At a time when I should have been happy, I instead was confused. If it was not my grades that was causing something to come between grandpa and me, what could it have been? Now I had no idea. I was never a bad boy, nor did I do things that could get me into trouble. I thought, what's going on. Maybe I should just drum up the nerve to ask him, although I know that he doesn't like being questioned by me. I tried that once and was told that it was not my place to ask or question what he does. Back then I wanted to go out with some kids that I really didn't know that well. They invited me to come along with them to town, and I wanted to go. Grandpa said no to that Idea. I questioned him as to why, and he told me never to do that again and sent me to my room instead. Well, my feelings were hurt, and of course I did what he said. I later found out that the kids I wanted to hang out with were arrested for shoplifting in town and got into a lot of trouble. I was glad I was not there with them. Grandpa was right not to let me go.

I went on thinking, this is different; this is between me and grandpa, and I really believe I have a right to know what I did or if I let him down in some way. My mind was made up: after I told him about my good grades, I was going to ask him why he was being so different with me.

We stayed at school for the whole day. I was able to see some of the classes I would be required to take next season. A few that were advanced courses that were designed to prepare you for college. There, too, was a class with my homeroom teacher, and I was excited about that since she was a good teacher, and I liked her a lot. Some of the other courses were led by teachers I had only heard about from some of the older students, who had good things to say about them all. I was sure I wouldn't have any problem with my classes or with my new teachers. And I could enjoy my summer off because I didn't have to attend summer school. Life was good.

CHAPTER 12

On the way home from school, I saw grandpa in the field. He didn't see me because he was plowing away from the road. I realized that it might not be a good time to talk to him right then. After all, he had probably been at it all morning and it could wait until later—there really wasn't any rush.

I got to the house, and Grandma Ida was sitting on the porch peeling green beans. I sat next to her and gave her the good news. "I got all good grades!" I shouted out. I wasn't sure if she'd understand the A and B system, but I thought it was important that I give her that information as well, so I explained that I received all As except for one B+. By the smile on her face, I felt that she must have understood something about what that all meant.

"That's good," she replied. "I'm sho yo' grandpa is going to be proud of you."

"Yeah, I hope he is. I saw him and wanted to tell him, but he was hard at work plowing the field and I didn't want to stop him, so you're the first to know," I said, smiling at her.

She smiled back at me before saying, "I can act like I don't know and you can tell him, iffin you want."

"No, you're just as entitled to know just as he is. If it wasn't for your great cooking and looking after me, I couldn't have done it. Good food equals good grades," I said.

Grandma Ida and I sat on the porch and talked for another hour or so before she was done with her beans and went in to start cooking dinner. I remained outside and waited until I saw grandpa coming down the road. He was sitting on the wagon with the mule pulling it. I watched as he went by the front of the house and on to the stable. I ran over to help him unhitch the mule from the harness and guided the mule into the stable where the block of salt and the feed was. Grandpa went to the backyard.

I was still excited and wanted him to know about my grades, so I blurted out how I had passed all my classes. I added that I made mostly As, which was about as high a grade as I could get. Grandpa was still putting things away and I wasn't sure if he heard me, so I said it again.

"Grandpa, I passed all my classes," I shouted, wanting to make sure that he heard me.

"I heard you the first time," he said, "and om so proud of you of yo' hard work to get dem good grades. I sho how it was you studied dem books dat what did it."

"I think it was more than that," I said. "I wanted you to be pleased with me—that's why I tried so hard. I did it for you too."

I waited for a response and could have sworn that I saw a tear in grandpa's eye before he finally looked at me and smiled, walking away quickly. That was it, I said to myself. We're going to hash this out tonight. That was not the response I was hoping for. I thought that he'd be more excited than he was. I even thought that he'd ask me about my plans for the next school year. The teacher had already been there talking about me and the possibility of going to college. No, this was not what I expected his response to be at all, and I need to know why he had not been himself around me lately. I could feel it, and it was not feeling good at all. He hardly even looked me in the eye anymore, and our conversations were short and nothing like they had been over the past year. Something had changed, and I need to know what and why.

. I went back into the house and into my room. I had to time this right. Yep, after dinner tonight, I decided.

Dinner was great as always, and I was sure to get my fill because I knew the possibility of me being sent to my room after confronting Grandpa was there. I stepped out onto the front porch, where Grandpa was sitting in his usual chair smoking a cigarette, as he did after dinner. I sat on the swing where I could look directly at him. He looked over at me as I came out of the house but looked away after a moment.

I thought for a bit before I began to speak. I wanted my words to be filtered and not in any way sounding as if I was questioning him in a rash manner. "Grandpa," I said softly, "have I done something wrong that you didn't tell me about yet? I've been trying to figure out why you're not…" I paused for a second before going on. "I don't know what happened that makes you not want to talk to me in the way you used to. I just can't figure out what it is that I did."

Grandpa looked at me, and again I thought I could see the hurt in his face. "You ain't did nuttin wrong," he said in the familiar drawl. "I jes been feeling a way since I got the letter from yo' mama: I needs to be sending you back up north soon."

I felt a sense of relief hearing that I hadn't done anything wrong. I watched as Grandpa got up and went into the house. He came back and handed me the letter from Mama. I read it through and handed it back to grandpa. In it, she thanked him for taking care of me and sent a ticket for me to go back to New York. I was excited thinking that I'd be going home but didn't see what the problem was. I'd get to see Jodie and Rosalind and Angela and Richard; I mean, it all sounded kinda good to me. After the visit I'd be coming back here to start school. I didn't see what the problem was at all. I thought, It must be that I'll be away when the summer harvest is ready; yeah, that must be it. Grandpa would be all alone without me to ride with him and help out.

In my excitement I stated that it would be nice to visit New York and see my brothers and sisters for a bit before coming back and starting school. After I said that, I could see a difference in Grandpa; he almost had a smile on his face.

According to the date. I still had a few weeks before the trip back home. There was an upcoming country music event, and grandpa asked me if I'd like to go. I quickly said yes, not giving thought to the fact that we had known about it for some time. I can't say just what it was, but grandpa was back to his old self again. He began talking about things from his past. I always liked hearing that stuff, and he made some things so funny that we both laughed.

That next week we did everything together. grandpa would wake me up so that I could ride with him to check the fields, or we'd drive to town to pick up tools or supplies he needed for the farm. One day we road on horseback around the land. It was the most fun I had had in a long time. Saturday was the country music show, and it was good to see Grandpa stomping his feet and clapping his hands to the music.

The week after that, I spent time with grandpa and my friends. Allyson was not as happy as I was about me going home to New York; she said that I wouldn't come back if I went. I tried to assure her that I would be back in time to start my new classes, but it didn't seem to help her very much. Gary was going to visit his grandparents for two weeks in Texas; he was leaving before me, so we said our goodbyes a few days before he left. Clarence wasn't going anywhere, so we did get in some pond swimming and some fishing.

The week that I was leaving came, and grandpa began to look out of sorts again. I figured that he was just thinking about all the work he had ahead of him and me not being here to give him a hand.

The day before I was to leave, grandpa told me to pack as much of my stuff as I could into my travel bag. I thought that was a bit odd since I would only be bringing all of it back when I returned, but I did what I was told.

Grandma Ida seemed to try and get all my favorite foods into those last few days. I was sure I'd miss her cooking; that is, unless Dad would be home while I was visiting Hew York. Allyson and Clarence came by to visit with me, and I assured them that I'd bring them something back when I returned. We had a good visit. It lasted most of the day, and although I was sad to leave them, I knew that I'd only be gone a short time before I came back and resumed our friendships.

It was here: the day I was to go back to New York. As usual the rooster woke me up and the smells from the kitchen told me that breakfast was going to be special. I walked through the kitchen and was a bit surprised that grandpa was sitting at the table as Grandma Ida stirred a pot on the stove. I said good morning to them both as I made my way to the backyard to wash up. It didn't take me long to get back to the kitchen and my place at the table. Breakfast was great: eggs, bacon, grits, and biscuits with butter. This was Saturday, yet it was a Sunday breakfast. Grandpa said grace and included a prayer for my safe travel. We all said amen and enjoyed the meal.

It was time to leave. I had to be at the train at eleven forty-five, and it was an hour drive to the train station. I gave Grandma Ida a big hug as she passed me the paper bag with food for the train. She was crying as she said goodbye to me. "I'll see you soon," I said her and thanked her for the food. Grandpa was sitting in the car and had already put my suitcase the back. I got in the car, and we drove down the dirt road and on to the highway. Grandpa was quiet the whole ride, and he had that look again.

1963

We got to the train station, and grandpa parked in the section we were allowed to park in. It was a distance from where the actual station was, but I did remember it from when I arrived the other times I had come there. Grandpa took my bag out of the back of the car and started the walk to the place we were to wait for the train. He still hadn't said much to me since the time we left the house, and I was concerned about why that was, but I again thought that he would be without me for the harvest, and he had the right to feel bad about that.

In the distance I could hear the train horn blowing. The time is here, and I better get ready for this long ride, I thought. We walked toward the area where I'd be getting on the train. There was another couple and an older man and woman at the place where blacks waited to board.

The train came roaring in, continually blowing its horn as it passed the area where we stood. When it came to a stop, I could see the other people getting on farther down; they were the white folks. After they all got on, a black porter approached us and let us on. I got on after the couple, and grandpa gave my suitcase to the black porter, along with something he put in the man's hand. Grandpa said goodbye and quickly walked away toward where his car was parked. I hopped up the step and onto the train; the porter told me where my seat was. As I looked out the window, I could see grandpa driving away. When he turned from me after giving my suitcase and whatever else that was to the man, I had seen a tear in his eye.

As I sat in my seat looking at my reflection in the window, I began to feel bad for both grandpa and Grandma Ida. They had both cried about me leaving. I felt bad about leaving them and wondered if they were gonna be all right for the short time I would be gone

As the train got farther and farther away, I realized that I was gonna miss Grandpa, Grandma Ida, and all my friends, but at least it was just for a while. I was also happy at the thought that I would be able to hang out with Jobie and see the rest of my brothers and sisters. It had been a while since I was around them. I wondered if they where taller than I remembered. I was sure that they would see a difference in me: I knew I had gotten darker with all the sunlight and exposure to it.

I finally opened the paper bag Grandma Ida had packed for me. The smell of the fried chicken filled my nostrils and made me even more hungry. I took out a piece and bit into it, searching for the corn bread that I knew was likely it the bag also. After I ate and closed the bag with the remaining food still in it, I let my seat back to rela. There was still a lot of travel left to do; New York was a long way off.

A few minutes later, everyone was screaming and running. I looked around trying to figure out what had happened, why were people screaming, what was going on. I tried to move but couldn't; I didn't know what was happening to me. I didn't feel any pain, nor did I see what it was that was holding me down. I wanted to scream for help, but no words came out of my mouth. I tried waving my hands to get someone's attention, but they would not move either, or no one seemed to notice that I was even there. Of all the people that ran past me, not even one looked at me. Not even one looked in my direction. There was something terribly wrong here, and I could neither do anything about it nor get anyone to help me out of it. I looked at the window, and there was no reflection. I knew that I should have at the very least be able to see myself in the window. I knew that I had seen myself there before. I looked again, and there was still no reflection in the window, not even of the people who were running by my seat. I took a deep breath and screamed.

I felt the hand on my shoulder and heard the soft voice: "Are you OK? Wake up. Wake up." It was the porter that had shown me to my seat. I looked him in the eyes and quickly turned toward the window, looking for my reflection. It was there; it had all been a dream.

"Are you OK?" the man asked.

"Yes, I am," I answered. "I must have had a bad dream is all."

"You sho did," the man answered. "All of a sudden, you began screaming and moving about. Tt was something to see, young man."

I felt bad that I had caused such a commotion but was glad that it was only a dream. I again looked the window. It was dark outside, and my reflection was there and so was the man as he moved away from me. As I looked at myself, I remembered the time before when I was going in the other direction. I remembered thinking that I was being sent away forever. I remember saying to myself that Mama was getting rid of me for some reason. I remembered just how bad I felt about the whole thing. I remembered crying because I didn't understand why she'd do that to me, cast me away as if I didn't matter to her at all. Now here I was heading back home to New York and feeling bad about leaving Grandpa and Grandma Ida. I was all they had daily. Mama had Jobie and Rosalind, and Richard, and Angela, and Harold. Heck, Judy and Mae were just a subway ride away. It's gonna be nice seeing all of them, but I look forward to getting back so that I can look out for Grandpa and Grandma Ida, I thought.

I reached for the paper bag that Grandma Ida packed for me and took out another piece of chicken and the corn bread I had left. And besides, who will Grandma Ida have to cook for like this if not me; I smiled at the thought as I ate the meal.

I still had some food left. Grandma Ida really looked out for me. I for sure wasn't going to be hungry. I resealed the bag and put it away. I still had many hours to go, and I'd finish the rest of the food when I got hungry again.

I looked back at the window again, at my reflection. It was then that I realized that I only had a one-way ticket. The last time I traveled with a one-way ticket, I was not going back home. I began to worry that this was some kind of mistake. I'd done a lot of traveling. At least once a year, Mama would send me away, whether it was to camp or Upstate New York or wherever, but I always had my return ticket. That is, except when she gave me away to grandpa. Could he have put my return ticket in my suitcase? That's got to be it, I thought. My return ticket is in with the things he put in my suitcase, and when I unpack, I'll put it away so I'll have it when it's time for me to go back.

I lay back and thought about the ticket situation before falling asleep. I was awakened when I heard the porter calling out the next stop on the train: "New York City.

Next stop New York City Grand Central Station," he shouted. I looked out the window and could see the tall buildings before going into the tunnel. The train car went completely dark for the time we were in the tunnel before I could see the lights flashing by. The voice of the porter again began the chant: "New York City. Next stop New York City Grand Central Station."

He than came over and took my suitcase down from an overhead compartment and carried it toward the back of the car. "I'll have this for you when you get off," he said as he walked away.

Now I became excited. I wondered who was going to meet me at the station: Was it going to be Jobie or Mama? I really didn't care which because I'd be happy to see either one of them. Maybe I'd rather see Jobie first so that he could fill me in on what was going on in the old neighborhood.

As I reached the door that led off the train, I looked around, hoping my brother was right there waiting for me. I stepped off the train and onto the platform and didn't see anyone there. The conductor handed me my suitcase, and it almost tipped me over. I realized I had never really carried my suitcase and that it was really heavy. I thought for a moment that I only needed enough clothing for, at most, just a few weeks. My case shouldn't be this heavy, I thought. I placed the case down and looked around. For sure I was going to need some help with this case, if nothing else. I still didn't see anyone, and at this point I didn't want to see Mama, because of the suitcase. I grabbed the case and started to move away from the train. I felt that it was not a safe place to be. And that was when I heard the familiar voice: it was my brother calling my name.

I turned quickly and saw him running toward me. I dropped the case as he reached me. I was so glad to see him. He quickly noticed that I had become darker skinned than I was. He noticed that my hair was an almost reddish color. I didn't care about any of that; I just wanted to let him know that I missed him. Life without my big brother was different. I didn't have him to go to for advice or to keep me on the straight and narrow like big brothers do.

He grabbed my suitcase as if it was no problem at all, and we walked the distance to the subway. I wanted to know about the neighborhood, but more I wanted to know how Mama was doing. We got to the subway car heading home, and I asked every question that was on my mind. Being the brother he was, he just let me ask and he answered as best he could. Mama was great and the neighborhood was pretty much the same, except that a lot of the members of the gang I used to hang out with were either in jail or dead.

He listed them by name or gang name. He explained in detail what had happened to each one; I could see that he was doing that on purpose. He wanted it to sink in; he wanted me to remember that it was he that told me not to hang out with those guys. He wanted me to know that if I hadn't been away, I very well could have ended up dead or in jail myself. I realized that he was right when he sent me home when I wanted to go with those guys to a gang fight or to do whatever it was that I would have had to do. I thanked him for looking out for me and for keeping me out of trouble. He went on to tell me things that were funnier, things that happened during holidays and concerning my sister Rosalind. I used to be the one that looked out for her, and he said he had just one situation where he had to tell some boy he'd throw him in the East River if he didn't leave her alone. She never had any trouble with that guy again.

We got off the train at the Eighth Avenue station and crossed the street to catch the bus for the last leg the journey home. It hit me quickly just how crowded the streets were. There were people dogging one another just to cross to the other side. I became unsure as to how I was going to survive this for the summer. I had become used to long patches of roadway that I could walk if I wanted to. Or I could saddle up and ride on roads and paths without seeing another soul. This was not going to be easy by any means. I would certainly be happy to get back to the life I just came from.

On the bus ride, I got the rest of the scoop from my brother and was pretty much prepared for the challenge ahead. Some of it I was not looking forward to, and other things I couldn't wait to see. Mama was the most important of all. I asked if her cooking had gotten any better; Joe just laughed. I took that to mean that it might not have. Mama was a great mother, but she never had to be skillful at cooking.

I knew that Dad was not home, and that was a bit of a sting since I hadn't seen him in almost two years. He had been at work overseas working as a chef on a ship. He was the main reason that Mama wasn't such a great cook. When he was home, the kitchen belonged to him, and I would be there with him learning while enjoying his company. He taught all of us that were interested how to cook, and by doing that, he assured we would take over when he wasn't there.

We got off the bus and began the short walk to the apartment complex. I quickly noticed the smells in the air of fumes from all the cars driving around. There was not the fresh air that I had become used to. Instead, there was the smell of gas and other things that I could begin to recognize. I also felt quite small surrounded by the tall buildings, all of which had been there all my time living here but had not until now seemed so overpowering.

We walked quickly. I believed it was so that my brother could get home and not continue to feel the heavy bag of mine he was carrying. There were a lot of people out, but I didn't see anybody I knew from my past there. I thought about my friends Andrew and Robert. I wondered how they were doing; my brother didn't mention them as he spoke of the gang I used to hang with. I remember thinking that both Andrew and Robert didn't like the fact that I began hanging with those guys and they made it clear to me that I had to decide whether I was to continue to be friends with them or not. I of course made the wrong choice, and now I wondered if I would be able to fix my relationship with them. I wondered if they ever wanted to see me again, much less hang out with me again. I wanted to ask my brother but couldn't bring myself to do so: the thought of losing these friends I had had for so many years was painful, and I just didn't want to hear that it was an unrepairable situation, so I just had to wait and see how it turned out.

When we reached the apartment building, I looked around at the courtyard where we used to play punchball. I remembered how we used the corners of the bench as first and third base. The middle pole of the small roof on the first floor was second base. I remembered the fun we had just in this little area. I also looked up to the fifth and sixth floors to see if Andrew, who lived on the fifth floor, or Robert, who lived on the sixth floor, was looking out the window for me. Neither was. They're done with me, I thought, and that's just the way it is.

We entered the building and waited for the elevator to take us to the third floor. We lived in apartment 3C, just round the corner from the elevator. I remember as a little boy hearing Mama say that we were in a good apartment since we didn't have to hear the elevator running all night and day. I was a bit noisy going up to the third floor, and there were more floors to go.

When we got to the door, I noticed that my brother didn't use his key to open it. He just turned the knob, and the door swung open. That, to me, was not what should have happened. We were always told to keep the door always locked and to check to see whom we were letting into the apartment before opening the door. I wondered if things had changed so much that we didn't have to follow those instruction any longer.

My brother stepped into the apartment with me directly behind him, and as I got inside, the shouting began. "Welcome home!" the voices cried out, I saw my best friends Andrew and Robert in the crowed of people shouting the words out. There was even a string sign hanging across the hallway with the same words. I cried.

CHAPTER 13

The summer came and went. There was no return ticket in my bags, and it was finalized when Mama advised me that we were going shopping for school clothes and to pick a high school for me to go to. I had a really good summer and truly enjoyed the time spent with my old friends, but it was time for me to get back to the country and that easygoing lifestyle. I had had enough of this fast-paced, run-everywhere stuff that went on in this big city. I also never got to really say goodbye to my friends, and I wondered if I'd ever get to see them again if I didn't go back.

The clothes shopping went well. It was always fun when Mama and I went shopping for me. I liked really nice things, and although she sometimes frowned at some of my choices, she always allowed me to keep what

I chose. The school search was a different thing. We went to several schools before picking the High School of Commerce, in Midtown Manhattan.

The first day of school, as I began to familiarize myself with the layout, I saw some familiar faces. They were from the neighborhood, and I knew that would be a good thing. The worst thing that can happen in a new school is to not know anyone. The next thing was to go over my class schedule; there I saw a bit of a problem. I was going to repeat some classes that I already had in my last school. For a moment I thought that a good thing, before I realized that I would probably become bored at having to do the work I had already done over again. I spoke to my homeroom teacher and asked if something could be done about the classes. She said that she'd see, and I never heard anything after that. I could only guess that there was nothing that could be done and I just had to do it all over again. I was surely not pleased about that but saw no way around my situation.

I only hoped that I could get through it and stay focused. Soon I would realize that I was not good at hiding my feelings about doing the work over, and cutting class became an alternative to sitting in class. That was when I got turned on to the hooky parties. We would meet at various places and party rather than go to school. There was a problem with doing this, though: the school would send out notices to the parents when we didn't go to classes. I got in trouble big time when Mama found out that I was cutting classes. If I was to be successful at this hooky thing, I had to find a way to intercept the letters being sent home. This took some thought and was a bit risky, but if I could get the mailbox key that was kept in the draw near the phone, make it home when the mailman came, get the letter out of the box, and put the rest of the mail back in the box, that would solve the problem. The problem with that was anyone seeing me during school time hanging around the mailbox was sure to question me as to why I wasn't at school or even worse, tell Mama that they saw me waiting for the mailman when I should have been in school. The conclusion was clear: I had to stop playing hooky and attend my classes, as boring as they were.

There was a toll to be paid: I became disinterested in school. It became a chore just getting up and going. The only thing left to like was seeing the friends I had made at school and hanging out with them when I could. Sometimes it would be after school in the neighborhood, and there would be drinking and other things going on. I remember taking my first drink of alcohol and feeling the difference it made in me. I was not so sure I liked it but thought it cool to do since my friends were doing it. I also knew that if Mama found out that I was drinking, I'd be in trouble. My brother found out, and after his words to me, there was no need for Mama to find out. He assured me that he would handle me if I didn't change my friends, so I did. I made it through the semester and got pretty good grades, even though I knew I could have done better.

The next semester I got classes I didn't already know already, but the enthusiasm I had for school was gone. I was on a quick path to dropping out. Then I met Carolyn. She was pretty and she lived a few buildings down from me. We began talking, and I was able to take her out after passing through her mother and the strict rules for dating. I missed her when I couldn't see her, but one day, there she was in my school. Somehow, she had convinced her mother to let her transfer. That made all the difference for me. I was back to wanting to go to school and to do good so that she would like me even more. A year went by before, for some reason neither of us could explain, we broke up. I tried seeing other girls and some were nice, but none were nice enough.

One day I ran into an old girlfriend. She and I used to sing together; she had a really great voice. I hadn't seen her in a while. She was a little older than I was, but we got along well together, and even though there was an age difference, she became my girl back then. Seeing her again brought back memories, and she asked if I would meet her that weekend. I quickly agreed to it and was really looking forward to it. She was always made-up nicely with facial makeup and really long eyelashes. She always looked like she was ready for her close-up on a movie screen. There were problems with her in the past: she was prone to doing things to hurt herself if she felt misused in any way. I remember people coming to tell me that she was walking in traffic and almost getting hit. I would go and get her and clam her down.

Friday came, and I received a call to remind me about our meeting. I affirmed that I would be there. Friday had been a busy day for me; we were expecting family over for the weekend, and I had things to do in preparation for that. Night came, and I was pretty worn out. I went to my room to lay down for a bit before going out to meet Barbara Jean. When I woke, it was past midnight. I would have to apologize to her for standing her up. I really hadn't wanted to do that; in fact, I was looking forward to seeing her again. I lay there thinking about what I could do to make it up to her until I fell asleep again.

I heard my brother calling me, and it got me out of my sleep. He had a strange look on his face when he told me what he heard had happened. "You know your ex-girlfriend, Barbara Jean?" he said. "She was killed last night. She walked into oncoming traffic on FDR Drive."

I burst in tears as I screamed, "No, no, God no. "My brother looked at me as if he had not expected that much sorrow. "I was supposed to have met with her last night," I explained to him as his expression changed.

"I didn't know," he said. "I'm so sorry." He left the room. He knew I needed time to myself.

The day of Barbara Jean's funeral was the saddest of all. I wasn't sure if I could get through seeing her, and my feeling that I was to blame was not making it any better. I began the walk to Third Street, where the funeral home was. As I passed the corner where the older guys hung out near the liquor store, I noticed that they were doing their usual drinking. As I got closer and could see the gathering outside, I stopped. The tears began to flow freely down my face. I could not control myself, and there was just no way I was going to get through seeing her lying dead before me knowing that I was the one responsible for her being there. I turned around and went back to the corner.

I could hear my brother calling my name as I awoke from my slumber. It was the first time I had gotten drunk. The last thing I remember is walking back to the corner and offering to buy drinks if I could drink also. When the bottle came my way, I turned it up as I had seen the older guys do and swallowed deeply. The first time it was the hardest thing to do, but by the time the bottle came back to me for the third time, I was able to get the liquid down without a problem.

"What happened to you last night?" My brother asked. "I was looking for you at the funeral."

"I just didn't think that I'd be able to make it through that," I replied.

"That's the reason I was there to be with you," he said.

"Thanks, I should have known that" I answered.

"It was a nice service," he continued. "Are you OK now?"

"Yeah, I'm OK," I answered, knowing that I really wasn't.

School had become difficult for me again, and now I had a solution to whatever problems I faced: I would find someone older to buy me something to drink and I'd get drunk, hoping that it would go away. Before long the solution became even more of a problem and controlling my drinking became harder to do. At the ripe old age of sixteen, I had become an alcoholic. I barely got through my classes, and my grades were falling to the point where I was just passing. There was one teacher who saw something in me that made her not want to give up on me. She told me that I could do anything I wanted with my life. She said I was better than I was projecting myself to be and any goal I wanted for myself was achievable. I remembered something like that being said by my grandfather when he told me the importance of going to school. There was something about hearing that from both my teacher and my grandfather that made it seem real to me. I trusted both of them and respected their words as true, as was the case with my father's and mother's.

My struggle with alcohol was affecting me deeply. Again, I began to lose friends; the older guys only put up with me as long as I came through with the drinks. My brother had moved out and was not there to help to keep me on a better path, and my ability to hide it was fading away. The only good thing, if I could call it that, was that I was trying very hard not to drink during schooldays, but the weekends were all mine to do as I pleased with, even if it meant getting into trouble with mama. I think that was what I regretted the most, having Mama hear about me doing something while drinking that I should not have been doing. She no longer sent me away after school like she had in the past. Maybe that was because my brother was not in the house anymore and it should have been up to me to look out for my younger brothers and sisters, which I did a poor job of doing.

Nevertheless, I was getting by, and that was all I asked of myself. My ambitions were few: I no longer wanted to sing at the Apollo Theater; I no longer wanted to write a great novel or become the middleweight campion of the world. My life was small, and I was small in it. Dreams were for other people, and setting goals didn't seem to matter to me anymore. My life was over. The thought of death came across my mind: Wouldn't the world be better off without me in it? I was convinced that my brothers and sisters would be better off, and Mama wouldn't have to hear all the bad things that I was doing in the streets. Barbara Jean did it; I should be able to do it also, I thought.

1965

It was my father's birthday. I was out with some friends; we went to a museum in Upper Manhattan. The day was a joyful one until I returned home and found mama and some other relatives sitting around the kitchen table. I was heading toward my room when mama called for me to come to the kitchen. There was something different about her tone, and I didn't want to speculate as to what that might mean. I only hoped that since my father was away and these were relatives from his side of the family, I was not going to hear that something had happed to him. I slowly turned around and walked the few steps to the kitchen.

Mama looked at me and said, "Your grandfather passed away."

It took me a moment to realize that she had said "grandfather" and not "father." I took a deep breath before asking what had happened. I was told that he had gone to his doctor's office, where he fell over and died. I wanted to feel good that it was not my father but couldn't help but feel bad that it was my grandfather. The man that took me around with him as he sold the fruits of his labor. The man that I saw every time I awoke when I was sick and bedridden. The man that spoke words of wisdom into my life, the man that drove for hours to get me to a good hospital when I was too ill to even stand up. Yes, he was important enough for me to feel a loss, even a great loss.

I excused myself and went to my room, where I cried. I wondered if things would have been different if I had gone back and stayed with him. I wondered what else I could have learned from him or if I could have become a farmer like him and eased some of his load, perhaps added some time to his life. I wanted to see him again and hoped that Mama would send me to be at his funeral; that would be the least I could do to pay my respects to this man who so changed my life.

I was heading back toward the kitchen to ask my question when I heard mama say, "No, Al's gotta stay in school."

About six weeks went by before I became very ill. I had the flu, and it was so bad that I could hardly stand, so I spent most of it in bed with a fever. One day as I lay there feeling just about drained of all energy, I saw angels coming through my room window. For some reason

I wasn't afraid; in fact, I felt calmed by their presents. As they came closer and hovered around me glowing, I felt that I was going to be OK. Then my grandfather came into the room. He walked right through the wall and came toward the bed. I remembered that he had passed away. I wondered what he was doing there. As he came closer, I could see his hand reaching for me. Mama told me a story when I was much younger: she said if someone that has passed away comes to you, whatever you do, don't let them take your hand. I again looked at the angels that were now right over my bed suspended in air and my grandfather, who was even closer than he had been just seconds before, his hand now fully extended. My mother's story in my head, I screamed out, "No, grandpa, I can't take your hand."

My grandfather turned and walked back into the wall he had come from. The angels glided through the air and went back out the window. I called out for my mother, who continually looked in on me. She rushed into the room, and I told her what had just happened to me. She smiled and said that I had done the right thing by not taking the hand of my grandfather in my dream. I never said it was a dream, and I never will. Mama took my temperature and said that my fever had broken. I wasn't so sure of what that meant since I had never had a fever nor been that sick in my life, but I knew that I felt much better and wanted to get up and move around. I had been in that bed for too long.

Under mama's directions, I took it slow. I was able to move about the house, but not yet could I go outside or back to school. That would take a bit more time and rest.

I felt a blessing on my life that I had never felt before that day with the angels and my grandfather. There was a purpose to my life; if there had not been, I believe it would have ended that day. A purpose that would be shown to me through my challenges, through my failures, through those I let lead me and through those I turned away.

I thought, there will be times when I will have to reach back for every resource I've ever gained through the people that I have learned from. There will be times when the patience of those who came before me will be the call I'll have to make. And yes, there will be times when I get it totally wrong and will have to suffer the consequence of that as my choice. Bur all in all, there will be a life to live, and it will be mine to do with as I choose. I could choose to live it for my own means, unlike my father, who made sure that the neighbors had food for the holidays. Or like my grandfather, who shared his crops with those who had little. Or even like my great-grandfather, who taught his children to care about others and to trust God for all things. And not to mention my great-great-great-grandfather: God only knows what his childhood must have been like, yet he found a way to freedom and became an owner of much land in a time when I'm sure there were folks around who didn't want it to be that way.

This is more their story than mine, even though it ends with me. When I look deeply at my abilities, I can't be certain that I would not have messed this up if I had been in a different time. I don't know if I could have tolerated being abused, even just verbally. I'm not so sure that I would not have chosen another way to handle things that would have probably cost me my life. They were much braver than I. They set aside what could have been harmful so that I could be here to honor them, and I do each day with the love I give to my children and to others. It is through them I am.

Yes, I very well could have ended this right there, but that surely would have left you in the dark about many things. I did marry Caroline. In fact, I married her twice, and I'll get back to that later.

In all I married four women over five marriages. I have nothing bad to say about any of them. The truth is that each one added something to my life that has blessed me. Please don't go thinking that I was running around just marrying women and divorcing them so that I could marry the next. That was not the case. You know that part in the marriage ceremony where it says, "till death do us part"? Well, that was the case with three of the four women.

Caroline I married twice, and she passed way. Dorothy and Susanne also passed away during my marriages to them, and one marriage ended in a friendly manner.

I have four children and eleven grandchildren and nine great-grandchildren, and only time will tell if it ends there. So, the family is continuing to grow. I can only wonder if Grandpa Philip could have imagined his family being so large, on my side alone. I still have a brother and sister with children and grandchildren and great-grandchildren. And sisters that have passed way who had children who have children and grandchildren. You get the point.

I received and honorable discharge from the United States Army and was able to go to college as a result of that service. I landed some great jobs and learned that I could use the teachings of my father and my grandfather in almost any situation. I learned to use compassion instead of fear. I learned that sometimes listening is better than speaking. These were the skills taught to me by them, and it worked with others as well. There was also the need to know that there was nothing I could do about some things, and I'd need to step away and do nothing. And there were times when just a little uplifting and a bit of encouragement made all the difference in the world.

Oh, if you're still wondering about what I do when things get rough—well, I pray. I no longer need to look for answers in the bottle. In fact, I found a real solution to the problem many years ago. And as I look back at my years, there are no regrets or hard feelings. I can understand why Mama sent me away. It was for my own good, and the time away was certainly not wasted; rather, it was a time to learn. The love shown me over the years became the pillar and foundation I based my life on. I know that love is much greater than hate.

I've spent a good portion of my life involved in finding solutions to problems that have affected my community. I've won awards and received commendations for my efforts, but what I know to be a fact is none of that would have happened without the men in my life who showed me the value of giving back.

These days, which very well could be my last days, I spend helping others. I run a not-for-profit organization that assists veterans and their families. I attend seminars and events where I can connect with agencies and create contacts that can help with this. I have a team of veterans and nonveterans who meet and discuss ways we can improve the lives of these veterans and their families.

I have a God who gives me strength, wisdom, and courage to continue on this path he has set for me in my remaining years. And I have friends and a church family that pray with me and for me. And I never forget to thank God for my ancestors, and the strength and faith of Philip, who passed it on to his son Philip, who passed it down to my grandfather Cleveland, who passed it to his son—my father Joseph—who passed it down to me. And yes, it is my charge to pass it on to my children and to let them know that we come from a long line of people who made us possible.

Every success I owe to them, for it was their struggle and pain that made a way for our existence. It was their torment that gave a path to my life. It was their prayers that brought them comfort day-to-day, and as I have grown in faith and in love, knowing this about them, I know it's not just for me and my family but for all mankind that I pray, Peace to us all.

Milton Keynes UK
Ingram Content Group UK Ltd.
UKHW030734121024
449407UK00028B/260/J